A PRACTICAL COMPANION TO CHILDREN'S LITERATURE STUDIES

A PRACTICAL COMPANION TO CHILDREN'S LITERATURE STUDIES

Conducting Research and Building a Career

EDITED BY

KIMBERLEY REYNOLDS, MATTHEW GRENBY AND EMILY MURPHY

BLOOMSBURY ACADEMIC
LONDON • NEW YORK • OXFORD • NEW DELHI • SYDNEY

BLOOMSBURY ACADEMIC
Bloomsbury Publishing Plc, 50 Bedford Square, London, WC1B 3DP, UK
Bloomsbury Publishing Inc, 1359 Broadway, New York, NY 10018, USA
Bloomsbury Publishing Ireland, 29 Earlsfort Terrace, Dublin 2, D02 AY28, Ireland

BLOOMSBURY, BLOOMSBURY ACADEMIC and the Diana logo are trademarks of Bloomsbury Publishing Plc

First published in Great Britain 2026

Cover design: Gita Kowlessur
Illustration © Donough O'Malley

A catalogue record for this book is available from the British Library.

A catalog record for this book is available from the Library of Congress.

ISBN: HB: 978-1-3503-7748-6
PB: 978-1-3503-7749-3
ePDF: 978-1-3503-7750-9
eBook: 978-1-3503-7751-6

Typeset by Deanta Global Publishing Services, Chennai, India

CONTENTS

TABLES

BOXES

ACKNOWLEDGEMENTS

Many people have generously contributed to the work of conceiving, fact-checking and internationalizing this companion.

Lucy Pearson and Karen Sands O'Connor both helped develop the original proposal and conducted a focus group with their graduate and postgraduate students at Newcastle University (UK), which shaped the content and aims of the book.

Research students and early career colleagues who are members of the International Research Society for Children's Literature (IRSCL) responded to questions about conditions in their countries.

The following colleagues read chapters and gave feedback to help verify and expand the international content of the book:

Nina Christensen, Aarhus University, Denmark; Macarena García-González, Pompeu Fabra University, Spain; Anuja Madan, Kansas State University, USA; Vanessa Joosen, University of Antwerp, Belgium; Regan Postma-Montaño, Baylor University, USA; Mateusz Świetlicki, University of Wrocław, Poland; and Fengxia Tan, Nanjing Normal University, China.

EDITORS

Editors' Biographies

Matthew Grenby is Professor of Eighteenth-Century Studies and Pro-Vice-Chancellor for Research and Innovation at Newcastle University, UK. He is the author of several monographs, including *The Child Reader 1700–1840*, and co-editor of books including *Popular Children's Books in Britain*; *The Cambridge Companion to Children's Literature*; and *Transnational Books for Children 1750–1900: Producers, Consumers, Encounters*. He chairs the Collection Trust of Seven Stories, the UK's National Centre for Children's Books.

Emily Murphy is Senior Lecturer in Children's Literature at Newcastle University, UK. She has published an award-winning monograph, *Growing Up with America: Youth, Myth, and National Identity, 1945 to Present* (2020), along with numerous essays and articles on children's literature.

Kimberley Reynolds, OBE, is Professor Emerita of Children's Literature in the School of English Literature, Language and Linguistics at Newcastle University, UK. She has won several awards and honours for her contributions to research in children's literature studies, including the Children's Book Award for both *Radical Children's Literature* and *Left Out*.

Senior Editors' Biographies

Tyler Bickford is Professor of English at the University of Pittsburgh. He is the author of *Tween Pop: Children's Music and Public Culture* (2020) and *Schooling New Media: Music, Language, and Technology in Children's Culture* (2017).

Shih-Wen Sue Chen is Associate Professor in Writing and Literature at Deakin University. She is the author of *Children's Literature and Transnational Knowledge in Modern China* (2019) and *Representations of China in British Children's Fiction, 1851–1911* (2013), and she is the co-editor of *Representations of Children and Success in Asia* (2022).

Elina Druker is Professor of Children's Literature at Stockholm University, Sweden. Her research area covers picturebooks, illustration history, modernism and the avant-garde. She has published and co-edited several publications dealing with children's literature, for example, *Children's Literature and the Avant-Garde* (2015) and *History of Swedish Children's and Young Adult Literature* (2024).

Courtney Weikle-Mills is Associate Professor and Director of the Children's Literature Program at the University of Pittsburgh. Her current work traces children's literature's responses to Atlantic trade and slavery, the circulation of British and American children's literature and the development of 'global' children's literature.

Xu Derong is Professor of English Language and Literature at Ocean University of China. His research interests include children's literature criticism and translation studies. He has published more than sixty academic papers in this field and translated over seventy children's books between English and Chinese.

Contributors' Biographies

Ani Rosa Almario is the school director and co-founder of The Raya School (www.raya.edu.ph), a progressive K-12 institution in Quezon City, Philippines. She is also the vice-president of Adarna House (www.adarna.com .ph), the Philippines' oldest children's publishing house. Ani has a masters in Learning, Design and Technology from Stanford University and a doctorate in Curriculum Studies from the University of the Philippines.

Charlotte Appel is Associate Professor of Early Modern Cultural History at Aarhus University, Denmark. She has published extensively on the history of books and reading, schools and education, childhood and church history *c.* 1550–1850. With Nina Christensen, she published *Children's Literature in the Nordic World* (2021), and a monograph and several articles on children's books and reading culture *c.* 1750–1850. With Matthew Grenby and Christensen, she also co-edited *Transnational Books for Children 1700–1900* (2023).

Ariel Baker-Gibbs is a Berkeley lecturer. She received her PhD from UC Berkeley, focusing on crip and queer theory, young adult and children's literature in the context of nineteenth-, twentieth- and twenty-first-century Anglophone literature. She is a Deaf ASL user.

Clémentine Beauvais is Senior Lecturer in Children's Literature at the University of York, UK, and a children's writer and translator, mostly in French. Her research interests include children's literature theory, translation theory, reading out loud and literary education.

Catherine Butler is Reader in English Literature at Cardiff University. Her academic books include *Four British Fantasists* (2006), *Reading History in Children's Books* (2012), *Literary Studies Deconstructed* (2018) and *British Children's Literature in Japanese Culture* (2023), as well as several edited collections. Catherine is editor-in-chief of *Children's Literature in Education.*

Katharine Capshaw is Professor of English and Africana Studies at the University of Connecticut, where she also serves as Associate Dean for Diversity, Equity and Inclusion. Author of *Civil Rights Childhood* and *Children's Literature of the Harlem Renaissance*, Capshaw is developing a book on Black children's theatre of the 1970s.

Minjie Chen is a metadata librarian for the Cotsen Children's Library, a special collection of international children's literature held at the Princeton University

Library. She is the author of *The Sino-Japanese War and Youth Literature: Friends and Foes on the Battlefield* (2016).

Nina Christensen is Professor in Children's Literature at Aarhus University, Denmark. Her research interests include the history of children's literature, picturebooks and concepts of childhood. With Philip Nel and Lissa Paul, she co-edited *Keywords for Children's Literature* (2021, 2nd ed.). With Charlotte Appel, she published *Children's Literature in the Nordic World* (2021), and a monograph on children's books and reading culture *c.* 1750–1850. With Matthew Grenby and Appel, she co-edited *Transnational Books for Children 1700–1900* (2023).

Sreemoyee Dasgupta is Assistant Professor of English and Comparative Literature at the American University of Beirut. Her areas of interest are children's literature, colonial/postcolonial studies, the long nineteenth century, popular and print culture and global circulation. She is currently working on a monograph on colonial Bengali children's literature.

Justyna Deszcz-Tryhubczak is Associate Professor of Literature at the Institute of English Studies, University of Wrocław, Poland. She is the co-editor (with Zoe Jaques) of *Intergenerational Solidarity in Children's Literature and Film* (2021), (with Irena Barbara Kalla) *Children's Literature and Intergenerational Relationships: Encounters of the Playful Kind* (and with Macarena García-González) *Children's Cultures After Childhood* (2023).

Anna Mae Duane is Professor of English and the Director of the University of Connecticut Humanities Institute, United States. She is the author or editor of six books, including *Educated for Freedom: The Incredible Story of Two Fugitive Schoolboys Who Grew Up to Change a Nation* and *Who Writes for Black Children? African American Children's Literature Before 1900*, which she co-edited with Kate Capshaw.

Marilisa Jiménez García is Associate Professor of Childhood Studies at Rutgers University-Camden. She is the author of *Side by Side: US Empire, Puerto Rico, and the Roots of American Youth Literature and Culture* (2021), which won the 2023 Children's Literature Association Book Award. She also co-wrote with Meg Medina, *She Persisted: Pura Belpré* (2023).

Lindsey Geybels (University of Antwerp, Belgium) explores age construction in fiction for different ages. In her PhD, she used digital analyses to explore reader age influence. She has published in several academic journals, and her work extends to children's literature and age studies. She also co-authored the book *Age in David Almond's Oeuvre.*

Anna Katrina Gutierrez is a professorial lecturer of English at the University of the Philippines. She earned her PhD in Children's Literature at Macquarie University (Australia) and has held fellowships at the Swedish Institute for Children's Books, the Hans Christian Andersen Centre and the International Youth Library. She is the author of *Mixed Magic: Global-Local Dialogues in Fairy Tales for Young Readers* (2017) and is a children's book editor and the communications manager at Lantana Publishing (UK).

Haifeng Hui is Professor of English at the School of Foreign Languages, Huazhong University of Science and Technology, China, where he also serves as the Director of the D(igital) H(umanities) Lab. His research interests include digital humanities and children's literature. He is a member of the advisory boards for *International Research in Children's Literature* and *History of Education and Children's Literature.*

Shuqin Jiang is Professor of English Language and Literature Teaching in the Center for Foreign Studies at Sichuan International Studies University, Chongqing, China. Her research interests include English fantasy literature, children's literature, contemporary English novels, narrative studies and translation studies.

Erica Kanesaka is a writer and researcher who specializes in the racial and sexual politics of kawaii and cute cultures. She is an assistant professor at Emory University, and her work brings together Asian American studies, transnational feminisms and childhood studies.

Helen King is a research associate in children's literature at Newcastle University, UK, with interests in the archives of childhood and child-adult collaboration. Her doctoral thesis explored the political potential of children's reading through the work of Beverley Naidoo, and her current work investigates children's contributions to community integration through their schoolwork.

Bettina Kümmerling-Meibauer is a Professor in the German Department at the University of Tübingen, Germany. She has authored four books and (co) edited 20 volumes, inter alia *The Routledge Companion to Picturebooks* (2018), *Political Changes and Transformations in Twentieth and Twenty-first Century Children's Literature* (with Farriba Schulz, 2023) and *Photography in Children's Literature* (with Elina Druker, 2023).

Gabriela Lee is a faculty member in the Department of English and Comparative Literature at the University of the Philippines. She is currently working on her PhD in English, focusing on children's literature and childhood studies, at the University of Pittsburgh.

Devika Mehra is an early career fellow and the 2022 Inclusion, Participation and Engagement Fellow (School of Advanced Study, University of London) for a research project investigating the role of children's literature archives, museums and libraries in promoting diversity. Her areas of interest include twentieth-century and contemporary children's literature and film in global contexts, critical archival studies and digital humanities, book history and children's publishing.

Philip Nel is University Distinguished Professor of English at Kansas State University, USA. He is the author or co-editor of fourteen books, including the forthcoming *How to Draw the World: Harold and the Purple Crayon and the Making of a Children's Classic* (2024), the first in the *Children's Classics, Critically* series he is co-editing with Melanie Ramdarshan Bold.

Lenise Prater is a teaching scholar in the School of Communication and Creative Arts at Deakin University in Australia. They teach children's and YA literature, and their research applies a queer feminist lens to fantasy fictions, exploring the ethics of interpersonal harm and violence.

Lisa Sainsbury is Associate Professor of Children's Literature at the University of Roehampton. She is Series Editor for Bloomsbury's Perspectives on Children's Literature and Director of the National Centre for Research in Children's Literature. Her publications include *Ethics and British Children's Literature* (2013) and *Metaphysics of Children's Literature* (2021).

Nithya Sivashankar is Assistant Professor at Texas State University. Her research interests include picturebooks about forced displacement, narrative theory, narrative ethics, peritext studies, and South Asian and diasporic youth literature. Her work has been published in the form of peer-reviewed journal articles in *Bookbird, Children''s Literature in Education*, *Research on Diversity in Youth Literature, The ALAN Review* and *Journal of Children's Literature*, and several edited collections.

Michelle J. Smith is Associate Professor in Literary Studies at Monash University, Australia. She is the author of three monographs and seven co-edited collections in the fields of children's and Victorian literature, including *The Edinburgh History of Children's Periodicals* (2024) and *Literary Cultures and Nineteenth-Century Childhoods* (2024).

Victoria Ford Smith is Associate Professor of English at the University of Connecticut, USA. Her work focuses on childhood and nineteenth- and twentieth-century British culture. She is co-host of *The Children's Table* podcast and author of *Between Generations: Collaboration in the Golden Age of Children's Literature*.

Lucy Stone is an early career researcher and recipient of over ten research grants, awards and accolades for projects on subjects ranging from medical humanities to war and forced migration. Stone was awarded a PhD from Newcastle University, UK, in 2022 and is currently a lecturer at Dublin City University, Ireland.

Francesca Tancini is Visiting Fellow at Newcastle University, where she has been Marie Curie Fellow with PiCoBoo, an EU-funded project on the role of colour in nineteenth-century picturebooks, in partnership with the Victoria and Albert Museum and Seven Stories, the National Centre for Children's Books. She holds a PhD in visual studies, has been a Fellow at Harvard, Oxford, Yale, Princeton, and Curator Librarian at Bologna University Library and the Zeri Art Library. She is a member of the Justin G. Schiller Prize for Bibliographical Work on Pre-Twentieth Century Children's Books Committee.

Ebony Elizabeth Thomas is Chair and Associate Professor in the Joint Program in English and Education at the University of Michigan's Marsal Family School of Education. She is the award-winning author of *The Dark Fantastic: Race and the Imagination from Harry Potter to the Hunger Games* and other books.

Lynne Vallone is Distinguished Professor of Childhood Studies at Rutgers University – Camden. She is the author of a number of books, among them *Big and Small: A Cultural History of Extraordinary Bodies*. She is currently working on a cultural history of the foetus.

Paavo Van der Eecken (University of Antwerp and University of Ghent, Belgium) is a PhD researcher who combines computational tools with close reading methods to chart textual and visual representations of age, race, class and gender in historical children's literature. His corpus consists of 1,000 Dutch-language children's books, published between 1800 and 1940. Paavo's research is funded by FWO grant 11N4623N.

Elizabeth West received her PhD from the University of Reading, awarded in 2021, for collections-based research in children's book history. She is a Visiting Fellow at Reading's Centre for Book Cultures and Publishing. Her monograph is titled *The Women Who Invented Twentieth-Century Children's Literature: Only The Best* (2022).

Andrea Mei-Ying Wu is Professor of Children's Literature and Taiwanese Literature and Director of the Chinese Language Center at National Cheng Kung University, Taiwan. She is the author of *Discourses of Subject, Gender, Place, and (Post)modern Childhood in Postwar Taiwanese Juvenile Fiction* (2017) and has co-edited *The Routledge Companion to Children's Literature and Culture* (2023) and *Border-crossings, Coming-of-age and In-between: Contemporary Trends in Children's Literature Research* (2022).

Yu Chengcheng is Assistant Professor at the Department of English, Faculty of Arts and Humanities, University of Macau. Her publications include articles in *International Research in Children's Literature* and *Children's Literature in Education* and a co-authored monograph, *Poetics and Ethics of Anthropomorphism: Children, Animals, and Poetry* (2022).

Dafna Zur is Associate Professor in the East Asian Languages and Cultures Department at Stanford. Her first book explored the contributions of children's literature to colonial Korea's literary and visual landscape. She has published articles on North Korean science fiction, the Korean War in children's literature and childhood in Korean cinema.

A NOTE ON THE TEXT

This book represents the accumulated knowledge, insights and experiences of many students, teachers and scholars at different stages in their careers and from a variety of countries. Not all of these are named contributors because we were helped in our efforts to make this as widely useful as possible by focus groups and discussions at conferences, through online forums, and by the panel of international readers who are named in the acknowledgements.

Despite our best efforts to be representative of the field, it would have been impossible to include examples from every country, language or tradition. Inevitably, the content draws primarily on countries where the study of children's literature is now well established in higher education. This means the content reflects developments in children's literature studies in the West rather more than in countries in the Near and Far East and the Global South.

Additionally, English was the lingua franca of the editorial team, and so all the contributors had to be able to submit their work in English. Despite these biases, we have done our best to give practical advice that will, we believe, be useful to anyone trying to build a career in this inexhaustibly fascinating field.

The editors would be pleased to receive ideas for expanding the volume should there be a future edition.

1

Getting started by Kimberley Reynolds

Although this book is about building a career in children's literature generally, including in education, librarianship and the creative industries, it is particularly focused on the academic side of this endeavour: what it means to study children's literature; how you find the right course; and what you can do with your specialism. Having decided to work with children's literature, one of the first questions you will encounter is 'Why?' This is particularly true of academics. Although the field became more established in some countries in the closing decades of the twentieth century, many people who have not worked with children's books remain sceptical about their merit and the value of studying and thinking about them (see Chapter 4). Individuals are attracted to children's literature for many reasons, but there are some compelling arguments for the value of this work that are common to all. It is useful to bear these in mind when applying for jobs and in interviews, since studying children's literature is, in fact, an excellent preparation for working across disciplines in academia and for many jobs in the wider world.

1.1 Why research children's literature?

Since all adults were once children and stories for children have been produced in the 'childhoods' of most cultures, revisiting writing for children as an adult can be illuminating at a variety of levels, from the personal to the national. Rereading as an adult a book that was loved or found perplexing in childhood can facilitate exploration of the child a person was. In the same way, because books for children are often used to teach the prevailing values and accepted behaviours of a particular time, studying the books produced – or suppressed – in earlier periods or at key moments in the history of a nation can highlight telling elements and debates from those times. For instance, under the fascist Franco regime in Spain (1939–75), many traditional forms of storytelling and writing for children were banned as subversive sometimes because they kept alive stories of national heroes discredited by that regime, sometimes because they validated religious beliefs and bodies that were officially banned and so on. Subsequently, there has been considerable work to recover lost and suppressed material, reshaping it for post-Franco generations of Spanish children. The children's literature that *was* produced during the Franco years tells its own story, too, of course.

The Franco government clearly understood that because children's literature is one of the earliest ways in which we encounter stories, it plays a powerful role in shaping how we think about and understand the world. Stories are key sources of the images, vocabularies, attitudes, structures and explanations we need to contemplate experience; because they are often bound up with education of one kind or another, they can be important carriers of information about changes in culture, present and past. Indeed, because of its long history and because writing for children straddles the domestic and institutional, official and unofficial, high and mass cultures, and often includes visual elements, material written for children can be a particularly valuable repository of historical information about everything from how children in the past looked and the environments they occupied, to shops, servants, the treatment of disease, religion, wars, migration, scientific development, exploration, politics and much more.

Children's literature's links to the past work at multiple levels, too. Just as the children we once were continue to exist inside and to affect us, so writing produced for children continues to resonate over time and to be implicated in the way we conceive, organize and manage societies. This is not a straightforward process; traditional ideas may be preserved in earlier texts or deliberately promoted in works that uncritically reflect current social trends. That said, many of the stories we tell children today are retellings of quite old stories such as folk or fairy tales, but instead of transmitting older values, their writers and illustrators set out to reveal, critique and adjust the matrices by which we interpret the world. The dialogue they create between old and new ways of thinking can be another way to sow the seeds of social change (see Bradford et al., 2008; Dixon, 1977; Reynolds, 2007). A good example of children's literature as a seedbed for change is seen in the areas of equality and diversity. In English-language writing for children by Indian writers writing in India and the diaspora, for instance, stories have promoted the idea of the 'new Indian girl', both representing girl characters as effective, admirable and powerful – characteristics that go against the grain of traditional images of girls in Indian writing – and encouraging qualities such as commonality and inclusion more generally (Superle, 2009). Children's literature has also been used to counter appeals to violent extremism in Morocco (Austin and Wainscott, 2021) and to challenge martial law in Chile (Faire, 2021).

There are, then, several ways in which research in children's literature can be personally rewarding and culturally significant – reasons that are sometimes overlooked by those who have not explored the field. Certainly, the reception of children's literature studies in universities has been mixed; individuals and institutions sometimes assume that writing for children is too simple and too closely associated with popular culture to warrant serious academic scrutiny. In 2023, an informal survey of students and early career scholars who are members of the International Research Society for Children's Literature (IRSCL) revealed that while those studying and working in countries including Belgium, Indonesia, Poland, Sweden and the UK reported success in building careers, bias against children's literature scholarship persists in many countries and institutions (see Box 1.1–1.3). For example, respondents from Brazil, some parts of China, Poland (there were varying experiences in this country), Romania and the United States have encountered dismissive, career-limiting attitudes to children's literature. It is useful, then, to know that precisely the characteristics that for some devalue children's literature as an area of study have intrigued many influential figures. Both Samuel Pepys and James Boswell collected chapbooks, the Grimm brothers' work on fairy tales was part of a more general study of the German national culture, while the philosopher Walter Benjamin was a committed collector of children's books. Benjamin valued children's literature in part for its potential to radicalize rising generations, encouraging them to resist established ways of thinking promoted through formal schooling. He was working at a time when artists across Europe were alert to the affinities between children's literature and popular culture, and this mass appeal was regarded as enhancing the rejuvenating but fugitive nature of childhood as it was figured in Modernism (Dusinberre, 1987; Reynolds, 2007 and 2010), making it a vital area of consideration for those thinking about and attempting to reorient culture.

For those committed to studying children's literature, it is important to be clear about its value and how it interfaces with many other areas of literary and cultural studies. It is a field that offers considerable scope for original research and thinking based on material that has never previously been discussed (see Section 2.1.1 and Chapter 5). It also underpins a great many careers, including those in education, teaching and child development, publishing, librarianship, museum work, translation and several of the creative industries, from film and TV to computer gaming. To give some examples, colleagues have reported that recent graduate and postgraduate students have gone on to work for/as (1) non-profit organizations focused on women's leadership and the defence of children; (2) some major art museums; (3) as illustrators; (4) a literary festival director; (5) school librarians; (6) editors or in other areas of publishing including as very successful writers (Gregory Maguire, author of *Wicked*, is a children's literature scholar); (7) a youth charity worker; (8) a midwife (useful, for instance, in countries with schemes to ensure babies are in contact with books); (9) a diplomat; (10) one works in TikTok's HQ; (11) another in animation; (12) there is a consultant for Netflix; (13) one is Head of Heritage and Culture in the UK Parliament (children are a significant audience for the heritage sector). Undergraduates who major in Children's Literature Studies have also used their degree to secure positions outside academia including in children's television at, for example, Fred Rogers Company and WGBH Kids, and in law (Senior Legal Council at W.W. Norton). As these examples show, Children's Literature Studies, which adds knowledge of children and childhood to other aspects of the arts, humanities and social sciences, can open doors to unexpected careers.

1.2 What do children's literature researchers study?

Students and academics who find themselves working with children's books and related materials for the first time are often uncertain about what constitutes research in children's literature and how it might be undertaken. Since many have already studied literature to degree level and so can be expected to be familiar with a range of critical and theoretical approaches for studying literary texts, this sense of uncertainty can presumably be attributed to the word 'children's'. What exactly is it that is being studied and where (if at all) do children come into the research? Such questions arise in part from the fact that in other areas of literary studies similar labels tend to be associated with creation: women's writing is written by women; postcolonial literature largely by those from countries which were formerly colonized and so on. Children, however, rarely write the kinds of materials, be they books, comics, magazines, films, plays, TV programmes or any of the other myriad narrative forms that are grouped under the heading 'children's literature', so in this case, the label indicates that what is being studied is a body of writing *for* rather than *by* children.

This distinction does not explain what makes up children's literature, how it is organized, what researchers in the field do or how they go about it. The answers to these questions are far from straightforward; one of the strengths of children's literature studies is that it is an intrinsically interdisciplinary field with many enriching interfaces with other areas. For instance, while many academic disciplines are defined by periods and movements (medieval, Romantic, Modernist, Aesthetic), place (Australia, Russia), genre (Gothic, detective, poetry), approach (feminist, postcolonial), or even limited to the writing of a single individual, the study of children's literature encompasses all such approaches and adds some more. One reason for this is that many of those who have traditionally been drawn to this field have come from backgrounds in education, librarianship and child development, each of which has its own disciplinary agendas. The reverse is also true: each of those disciplines includes writing for children and young people.

The breadth of children's literature extends beyond disciplinary eclecticism. The history of writing for children stretches back to classical antiquity (Lerer, 2008) and earlier, to the myths, legends, rhymes, folk and fairy tales originating in pre-literate epochs. It also takes account of contemporary and emerging trends, including narratives for children created by AI and online, some of the latter by children themselves, calling into question the notion that children's literature is written for, not by, children. Since children's literature encompasses every form, format, genre and medium, has been produced at all times and in all parts of the world, makes much use of visual elements, and is often taken up by those creating toys, games and merchandise, it is perhaps the largest and most varied area of literary research.

1.3 The child(ren) in children's literature

The term 'children's' immediately raises questions about which children are being studied: child characters in the texts? Child readers? If the latter, are these actual readers whose responses will be investigated, or implied readers, constructed by the narrative? And when dealing with a book from the past, which real readers? The original children for whom a book was intended? Its current readers? Or both? How old are these children? Does age matter? What do age ranges/generalizations mean? In the twenty-first century, children's literature is widely understood to cater for those from birth to the age when a young person is legally able to leave school. However, the precise age range varies from country to country and has also changed over time, so it is often useful to use the term 'Children and Young People' (CYP) when referring to the audience for children's literature. Naturally, the needs, abilities and experiences of this audience vary tremendously on age grounds alone, and also because the term incorporates CYP of all sexes, those from a range of racial and ethnic backgrounds, those who are physically and educationally challenged or intellectually gifted, CYP who are prepubescent and those who are not only well into adolescence but also sexually active, CYP who live in the countries where they were born in traditional nuclear families, and those – some separated from their families – who have migrated to new countries for a variety of reasons and who are having to negotiate both a new culture and language. This list is by no means exhaustive. Since it is rarely possible to make meaningful generalizations about the whole body of writing for CYP – not forgetting that a great deal of what the young read falls into the category of non-fiction or information books – those working in the field often find it necessary to specialize in writing for a particular segment(s).

The plethora of potential readers are all legally minors, setting up expectations that writers, publishers, reviewers and those who bring CYP and books together have a duty of care to their readers. This is another area that has raised interesting, often quite contentious, questions about what constitutes children's literature: what is and is not suitable for CYP in terms of content and language or what they do and do not need to know. Who decides this? Can a book that includes, say, incest, gang rape, attempted infanticide and abortion really be 'for CYP'? What about one in which the central character, a child who is unquestionably kind, good and innocent, is killed by 'friendly fire' at the end of a war and the incident is only witnessed by readers? Or a picturebook which explores the emotions of a father mourning the sudden death of his teenage son? These are all examples taken from books published for children in the last four decades, each of which contributes to debates about what constitutes 'children's literature'.[1] Such controversies are not new: in the eighteenth and nineteenth centuries, for instance, there were strong disagreements about such things as whether or not it was suitable to give children fairy stories and fantasy (Tucker, 1976). Reaching a decision about what is and is not 'children's literature' is complicated by the fact that understanding of what childhood is, how long it lasts, how definitions of childhood are affected by factors such as class, place, race and wealth, and what children's literature is for have changed considerably over time. This means that researchers working on, for example, cheap print, fantasy or Chinese children's literature need to be historians of specific periods, places, languages and childhoods as well as literary critics. Because illustration, including animation, is so often a feature of children's literature, they may also have to know about art, design, printing techniques and paper. Those researching topics such as representations of home, death and dying, climate change or place in children's literature may need to develop knowledge about childhoods across several periods, disciplines and even across countries.

1.4 Literature for CYP

Despite the difficulties of defining its audience's range and breadth, over the years some agreement about what makes a book 'for CYP' has been reached, though even here the ground is not always firm. For instance, do books that

[1]The books in question are Margo Lanagan's *Tender Morsels* (2009), Michael Rosen and Quentin Blake's *Michael Rosen's Sad Book* (2004) and Ian McEwan and Roberto Innocenti's *Rose Blanche* (1985).

find favour with CYP though they were not initially written for them become children's books – or, indeed, if a book written for CYP becomes popular with adults, does it cease to belong to the domain of children's literature? Whole studies have been written on the subject of such 'crossover' fictions and their implications for children's literature (Beckett, 2008; Falconer, 2009). Perhaps the most universally accepted advice about how to determine whether or not something should be classified as 'children's literature' is that given by John Rowe Townsend, who in 1971 concluded that '[. . .] the only practical definition of a children's book today . . . is a book which appears on the children's list of a publisher' (in Hunt, 1990: 57).

Townsend's advice may be practical, but is it right? Many researchers in the field find it helpful to look closely at how children's texts are written and the relationship between child readers and narrators; the work of Zohar Shavit (1988) and Barbara Wall (1991) has been influential for this kind of analysis. A more general attempt to identify key components of writing for children was put forward by Miles McDowell in a frequently quoted article about fiction for children. McDowell concludes that when compared to adult fiction,

> Children's books are usually shorter, they tend to favour an active rather than a passive treatment, with dialogue and incident rather than description and introspection; child protagonists are the rule; conventions are much used; the story develops within a clear-cut moral schematism . . . children's books tend to be optimistic rather than depressive; language is child-oriented; plots are of a distinctive order; probability is often discarded; and one could go on endlessly talking of magic, fantasy, simplicity, and adventure (in Fox et al., 1976: 141–2).

Evidence that much of what McDowell says is true of a great deal of writing for children has been provided by Torben Weinreich, whose research into what happens to adult texts when they are adapted for children concludes that the process invariably involves making works shorter, plots simpler and possibly adding illustrations. Does this mean that writing for CYP is intrinsically inferior to writing for adults? The assumption that this is so has affected the status of writing for children, which has battled against the prejudice that the nature of its audience dooms it to be simplistic and of questionable literary merit. Undoubtedly, much of what has been published for CYP – and the same could be said of much that is published for adults – does lack literary merit if this is equated exclusively with stylistically admirable, richly layered, metaphorically resonant texts. The reasons for this are many, but in the case of children's literature, there are some differences from sub-literary writing for adults, foremost of which is the way children's writing is often co-opted for pedagogic/didactic purposes. This does not mean that writing for children is innately or inevitably inferior to – or easier to produce – than writing for adults, any more than it means that all adult books are good books. Indeed, Jill Paton Walsh, who wrote for both children and adults, argued that children's books,

> . . . present a technically more difficult, technically more interesting problem [than writing for adults] – that of making a fully serious adult statement, as a good novel of any kind does, and making it utterly simple and transparent . . . .The need for comprehensibility imposes an emotional obliqueness, and indirection of approach, which like elision and partial statement in poetry, is often a source of aesthetic power. (in Meek et al., 1977: 192–3)

Compelling though Paton Walsh's argument is, the sense behind both McDowell's and Weinreich's views of what constitutes children's literature (that it is simpler, child-orientated, optimistic and so on) would have been familiar to the writers, editors and publishers who produced the vast majority of the material that has been regarded as being 'for CYP' in the past. Until the late twentieth century, they had their own unwritten ethical code that prohibited sex, bad language and depressive endings (Reynolds, 1998: 31; Tucker, 2006); to a large extent this code shaped the challenges to which Paton Walsh refers. Undoubtedly, the expansion of writing for teenagers (Young Adult fiction) has been instrumental in challenging ideas about what children's literature is and does; there are now many stylistically complex children's books that include sex, swearing, violence, and which end bleakly.

Current trends are expanding the definition of what constitutes children's literature (and so changing the challenges faced by writers and illustrators), but this new, more radical writing and illustration exists alongside the accumulated body of writing for young readers, which continues to be a significant area of research activity, adding to the large and mutable body that is labelled 'children's literature' and the opportunities it offers those who are researching it.

1.5 Choosing a course

As with every course in higher education, choosing where to study and to what level involves a mixture of pragmatics and desire. Inevitably, practical concerns such as finance, language barriers, location and family commitments will influence your decision; perhaps you need to live with parents or a spouse or maintain a job while studying. For those who are fully free to live, move and study, other questions arise. Ideally, you want an institution that has a good reputation for work in this field, with established scholars and excellent resources: some have specialist archives and collections or dedicated research centres to support original research. When you apply for jobs in academia, having studied with leading figures in your field always carries weight. Some courses are more established and respected than others, so it is important to do your homework, but obtaining a place on a prestigious programme is less important than finding a course that matches your interests, goals and the kind of researcher/student you are.

Interests and goals: Do you hope to become an academic? A librarian? A teacher? An archivist? Perhaps you would like to work for a charity or NGO that supports children, or move on to study an aspect of law, counselling or occupational therapy for which knowledge of children and childhood culture will be useful. Your talents may lie in the creative industries; children's literature plays a dynamic role in many of these. Your course should give you the background and methodological training you need to attain your long-term goal, so if, say, you want to use children's literature in a therapeutic context, your best course would probably not one that focuses on the origins and developments of writing for CYP.

Your research/learning needs: Know yourself. Are you someone who learns best from books, doing abstract or analytical thinking on your own (pure research), or are you better working with people in a live context, collecting data from, say, interviews or questionnaires (a form of applied research [for advice on the sensitivities around working with CYP, see Chapter 3]). Maybe you are drawn to research that requires high-level computing skills? All these kinds of research are explained in the following chapters. Check your course to see if it offers units that cover your kind of research and learning needs.

The delivery of research degrees varies from country to country, and you may decide you will do better in the kind of taught programmes offered in countries such as the United States as compared to the research-focused approach used in the United Kingdom. Choosing a course that will allow you to develop a profile in your area of interest, especially at dissertation or thesis level, is critical. If an institution offers combined degrees, not least with childhood studies, this can be particularly helpful for building a career. It is equally important to find a course that fits the demands of your life; do you need to study part-time or in the evening or by distance learning? If you know you require a social dimension to learning, the latter will not be a good choice for you, but many people are happy to study on their own, with support from tutors/teachers and occasional group interactions.

With career-building in mind, it is worth considering whether you will enhance your opportunities by studying abroad. For those who speak English, including as a second or third language, several European countries with excellent reputations for research and teaching in children's literature studies, including the Netherlands and Italy, teach some courses in English. If you speak, say, Spanish, but children's literature is not well regarded in your own country, could you study in a Spanish-speaking country where it is? This will not only give you the learning opportunities you want but could lead to work in the future.

1.6 Building a career by Emily Murphy

The world of work is steadily moving away from the concept of a single job for life. Increasingly, people's working lives comprise multiple types of work, sometimes serially, but often simultaneously. These can be complementary, combining, perhaps, teaching in higher education and academic support or work in a library/museum/archive. There are many possible combinations that will enable research and writing to sit alongside other kinds of work. As explained at the start of this chapter, Children's Literature Studies is particularly well suited for combining with other disciplines and professions, from education, publishing and the law to the media and social work. Since this book is primarily concerned with studying and researching in the field, we have provided some examples of early career scholars who are making their way in academia (see Box 1.1–1.3 at the end of this chapter); however, those seeking academic positions will also need to develop skills in working with business/industry/governmental and other real-world partners. For this reason, universities increasingly facilitate placement opportunities for research students that will be attractive to employers, including in the partner institution. Throughout your career, it is important to take up opportunities, gather experience and develop practical expertise, though you should do this in a coherent way that allows you to acquire real expertise in an area. Collaborating with individuals and organizations is another increasingly important aspect of academic life.

1.6.1 Collaborative possibilities in children's literature

As Chapters 3 and 7 attest, forms of collaborative work are essential to success in the field of children's literature. At doctoral level, you may be familiar with forms of collaborative work with your supervisor, whether that is preparing a funding application or drafting your PhD thesis. However, you should also be thinking broadly about what collaborative work might look like and how it can help you achieve your career goals. Some questions you might ask yourself are:

1. Why do I want to do collaborative work?
2. Who do I want to work with and why?
3. What are the benefits of working collaboratively?

Working collaboratively can provide enriching and exciting opportunities, exposing your work to a much broader audience beyond academia. To illustrate this point, we can consider two examples from the editors of this volume. In 2019, Kimberley Reynolds worked alongside colleagues from Newcastle University and Seven Stories, the National Centre for Children's Books to write and publish an article on augmented reality. This piece attracted a high volume of readers and citations, appearing in both a journal and published conference proceedings that expanded its impact beyond the field of children's literature and gave her work wider exposure. Similarly, Emily Murphy worked collaboratively with a multi-disciplinary team for a research grant entitled 'Beyond the School Gates: Children's Contributions to Community Integration'. As part of this grant, she co-authored policy briefs and designed interactive workshops with schoolchildren that included children's authors and illustrators. The creative outputs from these workshops were used to co-design, alongside children and practitioners in the heritage sector, a participatory archive exhibit. Such forms of co-research and writing are becoming increasingly common, even extending to publications with children and young people as a way of overcoming ethical concerns relating to adult-child power dynamics (see Section 3.5).

Collaborative work can go beyond publications, funding bids or conference panels. If you are someone who values this style of working, then you may seek or generate creative combinations of colleagues when forming teams to carry out research. 'Research', as I'm using the term here, need not be traditional in the sense of being focused exclusively on academia. If you are curious and genuinely interested in helping people, then you may want to see the impact your ideas can make on society. This could mean working with policymakers and practitioners in a diverse range of areas, from artists and archivists to charity organizations or high-ranking government officials. Such collaborative work will mean changing both how you and others think about what you do – how, for example, do you explain the value of children's literature studies to a busy elected official? It will also allow you to learn new ways to communicate what matters most about children's literature to you. By adapting the jargon associated with academia so that your ideas resonate with a broader audience, you will be able to form deeper and more meaningful relationships with those you partner with in your collaborative work, as well as see the impact of your research grow.

Another important career-building activity related to collaboration is networking: even as a new graduate or postgraduate student, try to attend conferences where you can meet peers and key figures in the field. Conferences can quickly give you a picture of where research is going and who is leading it. They are also places where you can be seen, establish yourself as working in a particular area and find potential collaborators, employers and colleagues (see Chapter 6). Organizations such as the Australian Children's Literature Association for Research (ACLAR), Children's Literature Association (ChLA), German Children's Literature Research Society (GKJF), the International Research Society for Children's Literature (IRSCL) and the Taiwan Children's Literature Research Association (TCLRA) all provide supportive communities and some also offer scholarships or other kinds of funding to attend conferences or undertake research trips [the IRSCL website contains a list of societies, resources and other useful information at http://www.irscl.com/resources.html]. It can be valuable to be involved with the running of such organizations, for this will teach you much about the field, help you develop and shape it and give you high visibility. There is no harm in standing for election to a committee as an early career scholar, even if you are not initially successful.

Careers based around learning and researching children's literature now come in many forms. Be creative, and never underestimate the benefits of the breadth and versatility of this field.

BOX 1.1 EARLY CAREER JOURNEY 1: DR ELIZABETH NELSON, AUSTRALIA AND SCOTLAND

I COMPLETED MY MASTER'S IN Children's Lit and Literacies at the University of Glasgow in 2015 and stayed on to complete a PhD around the topics of childhood and play in the post-digital age utilizing theories of children's literature, graduating in 2021. Two days before graduating, I started my job as Lecturer in Multimodal Literacies at the University of Glasgow, teaching on the Children's Literature master's and Erasmus Mundas master's programmes.

I know I was fortunate to find work so quickly, but this was not as seamless as it appears. I had been actively seeking employment in areas in and around children's literature for the year beforehand as my funding ran out in January 2021. I was officially on maternity leave from June but was actually working as an associate tutor in Education on a zero-hour contract. I started full-time work when my daughter was 5 months old.

Obstacles

- The position's precarity.
- Lack of maternity leave.
- Pressure to continue producing articles and grant applications when not being paid.
- Grants for which I was eligible to apply were all small, so I could not pay myself a salary; without an institutional position, I could not go for larger grants.

Advantages

- The extensive network of supportive scholars who advocated for me taught me about the UK REF system so that I could properly answer interview questions, read over drafts of resumes and offered to provide references.
- Knowing where to look for jobs and understanding the internal situation: this position, unlike some others I had applied for, was not effectively designated for an internal candidate, which encouraged me to apply.

BOX 1.2 EARLY CAREER JOURNEY 2: FRAUKE PAUWELS, BELGIUM

AFTER A CAREER OUTSIDE ACADEMIA as an editor, brand manager and high school teacher, a range of 'lucky coincidences' – and, clearly, my own wish to do so – brought me to academia: in 2016, I started a PhD, completed in 2021 and followed by two postdoc positions. Initially, the omnipresence of English as an academic lingua franca was a challenge to me. Even though my research focused on a Dutch-language corpus, doing a PhD required engaging with the often Anglo-oriented field of children's literature studies. Actually, this language struggle turned out to be a symptom of a larger issue: how to balance being present in the international field of children's literature with working on Dutch literature and building a network and expertise in that same field?

The latter was important to me as I want to remain rooted in my local community, but the demands of the academic system are difficult to combine with other engagements and outreach work. I deliberately chose a part-time postdoc position in order to do other work and activities that correspond to my personal needs and values. Building academic expertise was the gateway to many interesting things I now do alongside scholarly work, and I am grateful for this path.

BOX 1.3 EARLY CAREER JOURNEY 3: EMMA-LOUISE SILVA, BELGIUM

Obstacles: Transitioning to the field of children's literature studies for my first postdoctoral research project (after having completed a PhD in modernist studies and cognitive studies) meant that I had to quickly get up to speed with the relevant theoretical and methodological frameworks.

Opportunities: All academics benefit from mentors and champions; I was very lucky to have Vanessa Joosen as mine. She taught, encouraged and created paid opportunities across the three years of my postdoctoral work, building my confidence to submit an application for funding to obtain my own postdoctoral fellowship. Additionally, conferences and similar events have been invaluable. In 2023, I attended the International Research Society for Children's Literature congress at the University of California, Santa Barbara, and the International Children's Literature Symposium at Newcastle University. Each introduced me to supportive and constructive communities, such as the Global Network for Children's Literature which involves scholars from China, the United Kingdom and the United States. At IRSCL, I represented *Jeunesse* on the editors' roundtable, sitting with Roxanne Harde, Janice Bland, Petros Panaou, Macarena García-González, Åsa Warnqvist and Kenneth Kidd! I felt way less experienced than these rock stars of children's literature editing, but it was a great learning curve for me. Being involved with the Children's Literature Summer School at the University of Antwerp has enabled me to form networks with a range of those studying in the field since the summer school is low threshold and fosters a supportive, inclusive and equitable environment.

Finding work: Funded postdoctoral positions of one and three years helped me transition from being a research student to someone ready to teach in higher education. I am now Assistant Professor at the University of Namur.

1.7 FURTHER READING

Butler, C. and K. Reynolds, eds (2014), *Modern Children's Literature: An Introduction*, 2nd edn, London: Palgrave.

Ceng, G. (2021), *Ying mei wen xue yan jiu lun wen xie zuo : An li yu fang fa* [Research Paper Writing on British and American Literature: Cases and Methods], Shanghai: Shang hai da xue chu ban she.

Egoff, S., G. Stubbs, R. Ashley, and W. Sutton, eds (1996), *Only Connect: Readings on Children's Literature*, rev. edn, New York: Oxford University Press.

Grenby, Matthew (2008), *Children's Literature*, Edinburgh: Edinburgh University Press.

Hollindale, P. (1997), *Signs of Childness in Children's Books*, Stroud: Thimble Press.

Hunt, P. (1991), *Criticism, Theory and Children's Literature*, Oxford: Blackwell.

Hunt, P. (1994), *An Introduction to Children's Literature*, Oxford: Oxford University Press.

Lerer, S. (2008), *Children's Literature: A Reader's History from Aesop to Harry Potter*, Chicago and London: University of Chicago Press.

Maybin, J. and N. Watson, eds (2009), *Children's Literature: Approaches and Territories*, Basingstoke: Palgrave Macmillan with The Open University.

Meek, M., A. Warlow, and G. Barton (1977), *The Cool Web: The Pattern of Children's Reading*, London: The Bodley Head.

Mickenberg, J. L. and L. Vallone (2011), *The Oxford Handbook of Children's Literature*, Oxford and New York: Oxford University Press.

Montgomery, H. and N. J. Watson, eds (2009), *Children's Literature: Classic Texts and Contemporary Trends*, Basingstoke: Palgrave Macmillan with The Open University.

Pearson, L. (2013), *The Making of Modern Children's Literature in Britain: Publishing and Criticism in the 1960s and 1970s*, Farnham, Surrey and Burlington, VT.

2

Basic skills by Matthew Grenby

This section takes you through the processes of identifying, beginning, conducting and completing a major children's literature research project, such as a master's or doctoral dissertation, or a first postdoctoral project. It aims to help you navigate the early stages of your research career, from writing a research proposal to building networks and submitting your work.

The skills needed for conducting research into children's literature are little different from those used by any successful literary scholar, whatever the field of enquiry, and they are broadly similar wherever you are in the world. However, the challenges inherent in looking at children's books and other media do sometimes require that particular skills are emphasized, or that certain specialist research techniques and terminology are used. We have tried here to be as representative as possible, but cannot include detailed information or examples from every country. While the information and guidance here should be widely applicable, different scholarly practices are the norm in different parts of the world, so please do ensure that the guidance offered here fits the expectations of your own academic environment.

2.1 Choosing your project

2.1.1 Types of research

University degrees, especially higher degrees, are usually assessed by essays, dissertations and theses. Usually, these are comprehensive investigations of a chosen topic, based on both wide secondary reading and original research, clearly answering certain pertinent questions, presenting a coherent argument and extended to a specified word/page-length. The most common kinds of children's literature project can be described as 'literary criticism', involving discussion, explication, interpretation and evaluation of one or more texts.

Some literary criticism will focus on the texts themselves in detail, using close reading as its principal tool. This kind of work could examine the techniques an author or illustrator has used – vocabulary, syntax and imagery, say, or the ways in which an illustration, animation or film has achieved its effects. At its extreme, this technique can be very focused, concentrating on just a few sentences or one particular image and its accompanying text (cf. Section 5.4.1). Conceivably, a long, illuminating essay could be written on just the first line, and accompanying illustration, of *Winnie-the-Pooh*: 'Here is Edward Bear, coming downstairs now, bump, bump, bump, on the back of his head, behind Christopher Robin'. Such an essay might discuss (among other things) the techniques used by artist, E.H. Shepard, the tone Milne employs, the way in which artist and author collaborated, the viewer's place in the image, the various ways in which Christopher Robin's boyhood is presented, any tensions between text and image, the ways in which image and text work together to transform a maltreated toy called Edward into a cherished, living character named Winnie. To be clear, though, a research project would normally explore a much larger corpus of work than just one line and one image (a 'corpus' being the set of texts being subjected to study, typically those of a single author, or about a particular subject)!

Usually, literary criticism is concerned with meaning as well as method. *Explaining* a text is sometimes called 'exegesis', while *interpreting* it can be labelled 'hermeneutics'. 'What happens to the Hungry Caterpillar?' is an exegetical question, while 'What does the Hungry Caterpillar represent?' is a hermeneutic issue. This kind of interpretative criticism is often informed by literary theory, which provides terminology and models which can be applied to any text. Structuralist, Poststructuralist, Marxist, Freudian, Feminist, Postcolonial, Queer and Reader-response theory, along with other theoretical approaches that explore how texts work and what they mean, have all been employed in the study of children's literature (and if you want to take one of these approaches, you will need to make yourself familiar with its principles and practices, probably through reading specialist textbooks). Other literary theories have been developed specifically for children's literature, notably what is sometimes called 'childist criticism', which seeks to analyse texts in the light of the distinct abilities and attributes of its intended readers, and how they make meaning from words and images – thus repudiating standards of literary value that derive from an expectation of an adult readership (Hunt, 1995).

Alternatively (or additionally), Historicist or New Historicist literary criticism can investigate a text's context in order to deepen our understanding of it. Who wrote it and in what circumstances? With what events, debates and discourses does it engage? Some critics have argued that we should distinguish between books that *are* for children and books that *were* for children, and that the latter do not properly form part of 'children's literature'. After all, if it is the fact that children read it that defines a 'children's book', then books which are not 'written expressly for children who are recognizably children, with a childhood recognizable today' are not children's literature (Hunt, 1991: 67). Most scholars would disagree with this however, arguing that the history of children's literature is worth studying both in its own right and because it informs our understanding of writing for children now. Indeed, historical approaches are now prevalent, particularly for regions of the world for which histories of children's texts have not been extensively investigated. These approaches include histories of printing, publication, vending, reviewing, prize-giving and reading, and all the other processes that seek to understand full cycle of how texts work in the world, from production to distribution and to consumption.

Children's literature scholarship can take many forms besides what might be called 'pure' literary criticism. For example, some areas of children's culture have been so little studied that a survey, catalogue or analytical bibliography can be the most useful way of opening up the subject, and these will often be acceptable as a university research project. A survey of the books published for children in pre-Independence Nigeria, for example, could be illuminating, and lay a foundation for other studies. So too might be an annotated catalogue of the illustrations of a particular Aesop's fable, or a bibliography, with commentary, of children's books exploring the effects of climate change, say, or set in the Arctic. The same is true of annotated editions. Many children's books, both historical and modern, have received little or no critical attention, and it can be a very profitable exercise to establish the original or best text, to document abridgements and additions, to ascertain a date of first publication, to provide notes explaining obscure or difficult parts, and to add an introduction or commentary explaining the text's origins, reception, characteristics and significance. Equally, a comparative study of translations, both official and pirated, could be rewarding. Where manuscripts or draft artwork survive, the creative process can be usefully documented, and the role of collaborators, agents and editors scrutinized. Meta-studies of literary criticism might also be undertaken, charting (for example) the history of the study of children's film, or of children's book awards, showing perhaps how what is valued in children's books has changed across periods and between cultures (see Section 5.4.1).

What is clear, then, is that any kind of research approach used for literature in general can also be employed for the study of children's texts. That said, some methodologies can seem more specifically appropriate to children's literature. Considering books as visual texts, or even as examples of paper engineering, can obviously be important. Studies of a text's successive adaptations for different age groups, or in different media or formats – will also often make excellent subjects for children's literature research. As already suggested, reader-response criticism can be particularly powerful when looking at children's texts, given that children's literature is a subject defined by its audience. Very interesting work might be undertaken on how children respond to books, or what makes certain texts popular (or unpopular) with children, or whether certain kinds of material are appropriate (or inappropriate) for particular age groups (see Chapter 3). Looking at children's literature will often bring you into contact with other academic disciplines, notably the history and theory of education. Projects considering textbooks, for example, or pedagogical or paediatric manuals can be especially constructive, especially because such texts have often been neglected by literary scholars. Thinking about how certain kinds of literature can be taught in schools is another important dimension of children's literature studies. Work on children's and young adult literature is often more socially and psychologically informed than work on literature for older readers. You might choose to investigate literacy acquisition, or bibliotherapy, or how children's books have taken on religious or political functions. The study of children's texts is often highly interdisciplinary then, perhaps uniting literary approaches with psychology, paediatrics, linguistics, history, politics, economics, sociology, geography, law and children's rights, and many other subjects. Indeed, one notable development in recent years has been the rise of 'Childhood Studies' as its own subject area, in which approaches taken from many disciplines, of which literary studies is one, are used to understand the experiences of children in the past, present and even future.

These many methods provide myriad opportunities for research into children's literature. Often it is best to combine a number of approaches, but remember, just because you are adopting a particular theoretical or historicized methodology, you should not ignore the importance of close reading. Indeed, close reading should probably underlie almost all literary research.

2.1.2 Critical criteria

Today, it is widely agreed that literature should be judged chiefly on artistic criteria, although even this can be contentious. Are we asking all literature to break new ground, either in terms of subject or technique, or judging it purely on whether it succeeds within its own terms, or as an example of its genre?

Historically, and even sometimes today, literature is judged on other grounds: for instance, whether it is religiously orthodox or politically acceptable. Indeed, it is probably true that non-literary criteria have been – and remain – more firmly embedded in the evaluation of children's books than in material designed for adults. One consideration has been, does the book (or film, or comic, or game) teach the child anything? Another has been, is the text suitable – either for a particular age group (or sex, or class, or ethnicity) or for non-adults in general, meaning does it contain inappropriately 'adult' content? At least until the mid-twentieth century, the morality of children's literature was probably the central consideration of those adults who judged children's books, even for such apparently non-moralized genres as fairy tales, fantasies or adventure stories. This may no longer quite so obviously be the case, but it certainly has not disappeared entirely and book banning on the grounds of suitable morality remains particularly active in some countries (see, for instance PEN America's list of banned books at https://pen.org/ or Zoreh Ghaen's article on censorship of children's books in Iran at https://barnebokinstituttet.no/aktuelt/childrens-literature-and-censorship-in-iran/). Today it is difficult to imagine an author writing, a publisher publishing, a librarian or bookseller stocking, or a parent buying a children's book that praises bullying, say, so this issue of 'suitability' remains a major critical criterion. Additionally, values change over time and place. Whereas once, children's books may have glorified war and vilified pacifism, we are now more likely to encounter books that glorify peace and vilify war. Precisely what is judged to be moral changes, but morality itself remains central.

Thinking about these criteria is an important part of being a children's literature researcher. You may want to investigate the way in which judgements of children's texts have shifted over time, or between cultures. You may want to give special consideration to those texts that have bucked the general trend and perhaps caused controversy, expressing ambivalence about drug use, say, or challenging political orthodoxies. But you should also reflect on what critical criteria you are yourself using when you judge children's books. When you choose a topic, and as you assess your primary sources, are you considering purely literary or artistic merit? And what do these terms mean? Or are you assessing literature according to its didactic qualities, even if only in general terms? For instance, analysing a text's success in teaching a child about how to empathize with others for example, or how to develop a more positive self-image, means using its didactic force as a criterion. Or perhaps questions of a text's appropriateness are important to you, whether in terms of the intended readers' ages, or in moral, religious or political terms? Might you want to make it a principle that you try not to pass judgements on texts at all? There are no right answers to these questions. The criteria you use to judge children's literature will depend on the nature of your research project and the academic discipline that you are working within, as well as your own views. What is important is that you are aware of the criteria that, perhaps instinctively, you are employing, and that you reflect on whether these criteria are the most appropriate for what you want your research to achieve.

2.1.3 Identifying a project

The real challenge is choosing which project you will undertake. At postgraduate level and beyond, you will want your work to be original and to make a significant contribution to scholarly knowledge. Working in the field of children's literature this is often not difficult, since so much writing for children remains unstudied. Conducting a preliminary search of the critical literature will enable you to ensure that you are not duplicating research that has already been done. Looking at articles in children's literature research journals, and consulting databases of postgraduate work already undertaken will give you further ideas about the sorts of work that it is possible to undertake, as well as enabling you to choose less well-trodden paths. Reading some of the existing critical work in the broad area you have identified as being of interest will probably show you where the gaps are located. You might find that you disagree with some of the existing scholarship and so design your research project to challenge its assumptions and readings. While disputation with other critics is an important part of research, scholarship is a collaborative process, with each project contributing another brick to an ever-heightening wall. You should not get overly worried about the 'significance' of your work. Providing a reading of critically neglected texts, or placing them in their historical context, or assembling a bibliography of secondary work in the field, will often make an important contribution to the field from which others will profit.

Equally as important as scholarly value is a project's feasibility. Can the project be completed in the time available, and is it suitable for the prescribed word length of the essay or dissertation? Moreover, will you be able to answer the research questions you have set yourself? And crucially, will you be able to find sufficient evidence? This is always a major problem when working on children's literature. Even if you are planning a close analysis of literary texts, requiring no other data than the texts themselves, you might struggle to find all the sources you need. Many children's books from the past, or from overseas, are very difficult to obtain. Even major research libraries have not always collected children's books. Newer children's books too can go out of print very rapidly and become tricky, and expensive, to obtain. Finding data for other kinds of projects can be more difficult still. Trying to recover children's opinions of their books, for example, is notoriously problematic. For instance, while a study of adult attitudes to literature from the nineteenth century could look at diaries, letters and journals, children's views were seldom recorded; when they were, it was usually by adults speaking for the children. Obtaining today's children's opinions of their books has its own difficulties, raising significant methodological and ethical questions (see Chapter 3).

You should also consider your intended audience and the purpose of your research. People study children's literature for degrees in many subjects – education, librarianship, graphic design and literature – as well as for their own interest, and some topics will be more appropriate to particular disciplines. If you are a student, you will of course want to consult your tutors or supervisors for advice. Above all, you should consider your own interest in the topic. When you come to choose your research project, then, you should be thinking about four equally important things:

1. Is the project significant in scholarly terms?
2. Is it feasible, in the time available, and in terms of the resources needed?
3. Does the research suit the purposes for which it is being undertaken?
4. Will you find it rewarding and fulfilling?

2.2 Beginning your research

2.2.1 The literature search

As discussed above, part of the process of settling on a research project involves undertaking a search of the existing critical literature in the areas that you are most interested in. There are some standard children's literature reference works with which you may want to begin to ensure you have a familiarity with the general field you are investigating (see Chapter 1, Further Reading). There are also some online databases you can use to find more specifically relevant secondary material (Section 5.2 and Tables 5.2 and 5.3). Your literature search should help you identify what has already been written in your field and thus what criticism you will need to track down and read as you embark on your project. It should also give you some initial ideas about the arguments that you might formulate (although these will probably develop in unexpected directions as you consider your primary sources in more detail). The key thing is to be systematic in your searches and to take detailed notes to which you will be able to refer later on.

2.2.2 Primary sources

As well as identifying secondary sources, you will have to start thinking about your primary material. Your 'corpus' might be composed of easily available contemporary children's books or films, or materials straightforwardly accessible commercially or online, or they might be more difficult to get hold of – perhaps historical texts held only by certain libraries, or unique manuscript materials existing only in a particular archive. Chapter 5 contains detailed information and case studies about how you can locate, access and use this kind of material. But as well as these logistical questions, it is also worth carefully considering at the outset of your research the scope of your project and whether and how you will be able to access all the primary sources you need. For instance, if you are contemplating researching the oeuvre of Judy Blume, how would you find out exactly what she has published? Checking online bookstores and library catalogues would be a start, though with such a productive author as Blume, there is always the danger that you might overlook some lesser-known but very interesting work. And will you include her writing for adults, or concentrate only on her children's fiction? A research project organized around theme or genre can be more difficult to delineate and demarcate. How, for instance, might you identify all the children's films about the Cold War, or all the children's books published in China between 1912 and 1949?

It is essential to begin thinking as soon as possible about whether the databases and other research resources that are available to you will support the kind of search for material that you envisage. It will often be wise to set clear limits on your project, whether chronological, geographical or thematic. This thinking should be a vital part of your planning and can save you huge amounts of time later on.

2.2.3 The research proposal

Irrespective of whether or not your university course requires you to submit a formal research proposal, devising one is a sensible thing to do. The literature search and feasibility study are essential preparatory stages. Two other important steps are the formulation of research questions and a consideration of the methodologies you will employ for answering them. Research questions can be specific, general or a combination of the two. The sample research proposals below give some indication of what form these could take. Your statement of methodology should describe how you will identify and acquire your primary sources, and how you will interrogate them. Obviously, you will read/watch/listen to your primary texts, subjecting them to analysis. But what will you be looking for in particular? Will you use a particular critical approach? Will you attempt to place texts in their historical contexts? If so, how will you develop your knowledge of those contexts? If you intend to use questionnaires or interviews (Chapter 3), you will need to plan them at this stage. If you hope to understand how children in the past responded to their reading, what methods will you use? If you are interested in, say, diaries, are there enough you can access? Will you be relying on essays and books written by adults about the habits they observed in children in this period? Is such evidence trustworthy? Although it can seem tedious to do so much planning before you actually begin your research, bearing these questions in mind as you devise the project will save time later on.

Another thing you might usefully include in your research proposal is a timetable setting out when you aim to finish each component of your project. Whether you are writing an essay, dissertation or doctoral thesis – or a major monograph for that matter – you should allocate specified periods of time for each main task: identifying your sources, reading your primary sources, conducting interviews, travelling to a distant library, analysing questionnaire data, drafting each chapter, sourcing illustrations, attempting the introduction and conclusion, rewriting the chapters, rewriting the introduction and conclusion, compiling your bibliography, proofreading the entire work, getting it bound and so on. Having set rather arbitrary deadlines for completing each task, it is always tempting to think of the timetable as an aspiration rather than a firm schedule, and some slippage will almost inevitably occur as new problems and delays arise. But the most efficient researchers know that keeping to a realistic timetable is the best way to prevent a distressing rush as the final deadline approaches, and to ensure timely and successful completion of a project. The trick is not to make the initial timetable too tight and to set the parameters of your project to align with the time available. Then (however painful it may be) you should force yourself to stick to the deadlines you have set yourself.

It is often helpful to see how others have approached the task of writing a research proposal, so three samples are provided at the end of this chapter (Box 2.1, 2.2 and 2.3).

2.3 Conducting your research

In the first stages of your research, the two key skills you need to develop and hone are reading and note-taking. Both are more complicated than they sound. When reading/watching/listening to a primary text, you will usually need to think less about judging it than about how you are going to analyse and interpret it. When you *analyse* primary material, you are breaking it down into its literary ingredients, so to speak, and examining the relationship between them, or considering how these constituent parts generate the overall effect of the text. *Interpretation* is more concerned with setting out its meanings. Reading secondary material requires more *evaluation*. Do you agree with the critics? Is there something missing in their analyses that you can add? Whether reading primary or secondary material, your key task is to pick out the constituents that are germane to your project. As you use each text, you should note down details of your analysis, interpretation and evaluation to reflect on later, and draw links between the different texts you consult. Concisely summarize the text – the plot of a novel, say, or the argument of a critic – rather than merely restating it. You will also want to draw out those aspects of the text that are relevant to your argument, recording them for further consideration and perhaps also discussing them in your notes. You might want to record quotations from the text. You should also record your reactions to what you are reading – the shortcomings of a work of criticism, say, or how you think the text fits into your developing argument.

Ideally, you will use a computer for all your note-taking. Editing your notes is much easier on a screen than on the page, and being able to copy data from one file to another is very advantageous. For one thing, you can save time by cutting and pasting material from your notes into your drafts; for another, you can easily make backup copies ensuring that you never lose all of your work. If you need to take notes by hand, the same basic principles apply. Start a new computer file or notebook page for each new source and transcribe the full bibliographic details as soon as you begin to examine the text. Alternatively, you can use a commercial citation and reference management tool (e.g. 'Endnote', 'Mendeley' or 'Zotero').

However you keep your notes, record the following details (as appropriate to the kind of source you are using), most of which you will need when you compile your bibliography:

- author, illustrator and, for films, director
- title, including full subtitles
- title of journal (or book series) plus volume and issue number
- date of first publication and date of the edition you are using
- publisher and place of publication
- author, title and page numbers of individual essays in a journal or collection of essays
- catalogue number of a manuscript, plus the name of the collection from which it comes and, for correspondence, the recipient and date
- for internet texts: the Unique Resource Locator (URL) and the date that you accessed the material (websites are prone to evolve or disappear), plus the website's title and author if available
- where you encountered the text (library and shelfmark, for instance, or the name of the online database)

Some of these elements may be hard to find.

The accuracy of notes is important: you do not want to waste time later by going back to re-check. Copy out quotations precisely, retaining any errors if they appear in the original quotation (which you signify by adding '[*sic*]', meaning 'thus'). Record the page numbers of any relevant information, even if you are not quoting verbatim. If a quotation runs from one page onto another, note this in your transcription using a vertical line to mark the page break ('|'). If eventually you use only part of the quotation, you will know where, within a page range, that snippet occurred. Use ellipses in square brackets ('[. . .]') to show where you have omitted words from your transcription of a quotation. If you are using an audio or video recording, recording the time code or scene number allows you to return quickly to the relevant place.

Well-honed note-taking skills will be particularly useful if, as is likely, you have to visit a library or other research institution located some distance away (Chapter 5). Your time there will probably be limited, and you may not be able to return to supplement or verify your notes. The following chapters discuss different forms of research. Whatever form your research takes, how you file your notes is important. One tactic is to start separate files for particular themes, or 'work packages', or for each of your chapters, perhaps.

2.3.1 Turning an idea into a thesis

While formulating your research proposal and collecting your data, you also need to advance various hypotheses about your subject. Once you have a reasonable corpus of evidence from both primary and secondary sources and have thought about how it relates to your research questions, you will need to develop an overall argument, or thesis. Almost all successful pieces of research attempt to prove (or disprove) a particular point, or series of linked points. All the data that you have collected – whether from your readings of the texts and their contexts, from questionnaires, or from applying particular theories/ approaches – constitute evidence to support your thesis. You need to construct a *case*, much as a lawyer would do in a court case, marshalling and presenting your evidence. You might raise possible objections to your case, but only to confront and refute them. Indeed, acknowledging the complexity of the issues, and admitting the force of counterarguments will strengthen, not weaken, your work. An argument can extend over a whole thesis, perhaps consisting of smaller, discrete arguments concatenated together. Remember, no matter how insightful your analysis, simply *describing* or *discussing* a topic without reaching any conclusions will not result in a good dissertation or thesis. But you should also avoid being too opinionated. Presenting emphatic arguments is only good if your conclusions have been proved through deployment and discussion of the evidence.

2.4 Writing up your research

2.4.1 Writing a draft

Once you near the end of your research, or some aspect of it, you will be ready to start writing a draft. Start by returning to the chapter outline you produced for your research proposal; does it still hold good, or should the structure be modified in light of what you have discovered? Each chapter should both make a separate argument and contribute to the dissertation's/thesis's overall case. Before you begin writing, you might want to make sure that your argument holds water. Talk about it with your supervisors and fellow students; perhaps present your ideas to a work-in-progress group at your institution or test them in an online discussion group.

Isolating your principal arguments will enable you to determine which parts of your research are relevant and which are superfluous. Ideally, your research will have uncovered interesting things and underpinned pioneering readings of your primary material. You might think that all of these things are worthy of being brought to wider attention; alas, any essay, dissertation, thesis or book, must remain focused, so if something does not contribute to your central case, it should be excluded or saved for another project. Knowing what to leave out is one of the hardest skills to learn.

While writing your draft chapters, keep your intended readership in mind. This helps to determine the right tone and level at which you should pitch the work. Students sometimes imagine that they are writing only for their supervisors and examiners, but it is to be hoped that other readers, less familiar with the subject, will pick up a dissertation/thesis and any publications that stem from it. Try to ensure that even someone who has never studied your subject before can understand and enjoy reading your research. Indeed, after all your research, it is almost certain that *none* of your readers will know as much about the subject as you, so explain the basics – although this probably won't include plot summaries, biographical information about authors and illustrators, surveys of the contexts in which texts were produced and other background facts which are well known or easily available.

Before you begin writing, you may find it helpful to set down a section-by-section (or even paragraph-by-paragraph) plan of what you want to say. This does not mean you must write each chapter in order; indeed, introductory and concluding sections are often better written after everything else has been completed. As you progress from one stage of your argument to the next, you will want to explain clearly how one point leads to the next, why you are changing tack, and to remind the reader of how the points you are making fit into the overall argument. Such 'signposting' not only helps readers but will encourage you to think about how your draft fits together and builds towards its final goals. It is probably best to write your first draft quickly – time spent honing a phrase is wasted if you eventually omit this part of your work. Even at this stage you should include full citations for any material that you refer to or quote; otherwise, there is the danger that you will have to spend a great deal of time later trying to relocate bibliographic information and page numbers.

2.4.2 Citation in children's literature studies

You will save time by ensuring that your references are in line with the specific citation format required by your institution. As noted above, a reference management tool can help you with this, allowing you to generate references and a bibliography in any format from the bibliographical details you have logged during your research. Your department will sometimes have its own lengthy style guide, which will govern everything from the proper form in which references, book titles, dates and so on should appear, to the physical appearance of the text (things like margins, font size, line-spacing and so on). Alternatively, you might be required to use one of the widely used referencing systems, such as those set out by the Modern Humanities Research Association (MHRA: https://www.mhra.org.uk/style/) or the Modern Language Association (MLA: www.mla.org/). If there is no guidance about which you should use, choose a system. In all cases, the most important thing is to choose one style and stick to it.

The purpose of providing references for any material you quote, paraphrase or discuss in detail, other than to avoid accusations of plagiarism, is to help later researchers to find the material to which you are referring. Working with children's literature, however, can raise some specialized referencing issues. One common problem is that many children's books – especially older material, books designed for the very young, ephemeral productions and picturebooks – are unpaginated. In these cases, one way to provide readers with a page number is to count the number of pages yourself, using lower-case Roman numerals for any material before the main text starts (the title page is often 'p.i'), and then Arabic numerals for the main text (beginning afresh with 'p.1'). When you refer to a particular page, place the numerals in square brackets to show that the page number is not actually given in the text: 'p.[ix]' or 'pp.[23–24]'. When this is not possible, for instance with very long works, you can simply note that the work is 'unpaged' and perhaps add a note of the section of the book (e.g. 'Chapter 32').

Improvising references is often necessary when working with children's literature. The major referencing systems will not tell you, for instance, how to cite a paper doll that comes with a book and is supposed to be placed by the reader in the illustration on every page opening. Nor do systems always cope well with the paratextual playfulness that has become such a feature of picturebooks: deliberately disrupted pagination, prefaces appearing at the end of a book, text printed upside down, or on the book's covers and so on. You will have to decide how best to cite unconventional material, aiming always for clarity and conciseness. The terms 'recto' and 'verso' may be useful to designate the front and back of a page respectively (i.e. to say the right- and left-hand page of a book as one reads it).

Problems also commonly arise from publishers' apparent belief that it is not necessary to print full bibliographic details in children's books. Many children's books, both historical and modern, are undated and have no place of publication, but you should include both the date of first publication and the date of the edition that you are using in your citations and bibliography. Dates of first publication can often be found in the standard reference resources or online, but some may have to be estimated. You should make it clear if you have estimated a date by adding the word '*circa*' (or the abbreviation 'c.') before the year, or by using a formula like this: 'no date but c.1930'. You might base your own estimate on the information given in catalogues, or on ancillary data such as a dated inscription, or the years in which a publishing house is known to have been operating, or a reference to a particular event in the text itself. If you can work out the date exactly, but it is not actually given in the book, you can place it in square brackets: '[1930]'.

Children's book publishers also tend to be lax about noting changes made in new editions of a work. They are prone to change the illustrations, abridge texts or even rename characters and revise plots, without acknowledgement, often with the intention of erasing phrases or attitudes thought to be unsuitable for modern children. This is true across all media: films can be cut, websites changed, picturebooks reformatted, television programmes altered for broadcast in different countries and so on. This is why you need to be very careful when choosing which versions of a work to use in your research. Certainly, you should make it clear in your references which version(s) of a text you are using, differentiating where necessary between successive editions, or different translations, or versions produced for different age groups. Tracing such evolutions can be tremendously interesting and instructive, but it may be arduous.

2.4.3 Quotation

The evidence you present to support your case might take many different forms, but the most common technique in our field is to quote, either from primary or secondary texts. Although it is a fundamental skill, quotation is often done poorly. One rule is not to include more of a quotation than is necessary to make your point. You should usually feel free to start a quotation in mid-sentence and to omit irrelevant parts, using ellipsis ('[. . .]'). Ideally, most quotations will be integrated into your own prose. Above all, quotations should always illustrate a particular point that you expand on in your own words. Introduce a longer quotation, perhaps remarking on it in general terms, then comment on it in more detail. Here is an example of good practice:

> Having explained that Belladonna Took's youthful 'adventures' made her 'not entirely hobbitlike', Tolkien assures us that she became much more domesticated after she married Bilbo's father, Bungo Baggins: 'Bungo [. . .] built the most luxurious hobbit-hole for her (and partly with her money) that was to be found [. . .], and there they remained to the end of their days.' (p.8) By showing us the tranquilising, but also perhaps restricting, effect of affluence, and particularly the effect of appropriated wealth (Bungo uses '*her* money'), Tolkien carefully plants the idea that prosperity, especially when based on expropriation, must always be enervating and constraining – something borne out later in the novel by the dragon Smaug and Bilbo's own experiences.

Of course, you should provide a citation for any quoted material, using your referencing system. Always supply citations, even for material that you are paraphrasing, not directly quoting.

Quoting other critics is sometimes useful, but paraphrasing their ideas, or rather summarizing them, is often more appropriate. Whether you précis or quote directly, you should only use the ideas of critics to help you make your own argument, and never to make your argument for you. It is often worthwhile to quote a short passage of criticism in order to disagree with or explain how it needs modification. For example (this time using Tolkien as a critic, not an author):

> Tolkien believed that towards the end of fairy tales we usually find a 'sudden turn', at which point 'we get a piercing glimpse of joy, and heart's desire, that for a moment passes outside the frame, rends indeed the very web of story, and lets a gleam come through.' While he was able to demonstrate this to be the case with several traditional tales, many more recent fairy stories deliberately attempt to break the 'web of story' at the outset by showing the artificiality of the division between the fantasy world and our own.

This said, it is sometimes tempting to seek corroboration of your own findings from other authors or critics ('Diana Wynne Jones has acknowledged that, as I have argued, her fantasy literature diverges from the principles set out by Tolkien'). If you do this, remember that such endorsements provide only *support* for your view, not *proof* that you are right.

2.4.4 Using literary theory

Literary theory is not something that, in itself, can provide proof that your argument is right. Nor is theory a sort of machine into which you can feed a text and wait for the correct interpretation to emerge at the other end. Nor should theory be used merely to embellish your work; bolting on a theoretical reading will not make your research look more 'weighty', and sprinkling theoretical terminology around to no purpose will undermine rather than improve your research. In other words, only use literary theory when it is appropriate for the research questions that you have set yourself.

That said, literary theory need not inspire trepidation. After all, when working on children's literature it is almost impossible to avoid taking some kind of theoretical stance. Thinking about the age of the intended or implied reader, as most children's book critics do in some way, necessarily relies on a kind of reader-response criticism. Wrestling with the complications that arise from the fact that one group – adults – writes books for another – children – inevitably raises theoretical issues. Some critics have seen this as a form of 'colonial' relationship, arguing that postcolonial theory is helpful when thinking about how adults use literature to exert cultural power over children (this view has been contested). It is perfectly legitimate to employ theory as one tool among many that you use in your project, to mix theories, and to combine theoretical readings with more traditional close reading practices. The key thing to remember is that, unless you are writing specifically *about* literary theory, then theory is a tool for your analysis, not an end in itself.

2.4.5 Using Generative AI

At the time of writing, the use of Artificial Intelligence (AI) in research is in a relatively early stage, and its implications are still being worked out. Generative AI, such as OpenAI's Chat GPT, Microsoft's Copilot or Google's Gemini, can create text (or other content) according to the prompts given, relying on an enormous corpus of underlying material on which it has been trained. One of these systems could be prompted to: 'Write a dissertation chapter of 5,000 words about Gothic elements in modern children's literature, paying particular attention to female characters and making reference to at least ten different books'. Results arrive in seconds, but are variable in quality (depending on the Large Language Model underlying the AI and specificity of the prompts), but these systems are rapidly improving. Naturally, there is a concern that students or indeed established academics will use Generative AI instead of producing their own work. Simply reproducing content generated by AI and passing it off as one's own work is plagiarism and will be regarded as a serious academic offence. But the AI genie cannot be put back into the bottle, and institutions are now focusing on how AI can be used constructively as part of the research process, rather than seeking to ban its use.

While you should certainly not use AI to write your work for you, it does have valuable and legitimate uses. It can be useful as you undertake your preparatory reading. If you feed in a longer text, it can provide a summary, precis or translation. Then as you begin to marshal your ideas, you could ask AI to kick-start your thinking, either with some text in response to a general prompt, or with a suggested chapter breakdown. You could then critique and amend what has been generated. It can be useful as you are writing, too. If you become blocked (at the start of a new section, say) you could ask AI for some text on your topic which will give you something to react to. If you ask it to paraphrase your ideas in a certain style, it can show you how your thinking could be presented in different and more effective ways. AI can also check your grammar and spelling. The point is, to use AI interactively, rather than to do your work for you. Just as your questions prompt its responses, its responses can prompt you to think creatively and critically about how to develop your writing.

AI does need to be used with caution. Your institution, or perhaps a journal in which you are hoping to publish your work, may have its own rules about AI. You may for instance be required to acknowledge and cite your use of AI in certain ways (and this is good practice generally). Remember that the information returned by AI may be false, or biased. The Large Language Models on which they draw are usually scraped from the internet, with no particular quality control. Online information about children's literature is often opinionated and variable in quality (and some elements of children's literature are not extensively covered online). At the time of writing, generative AI models are being criticized for 'inventing' quotations and citations. This will change as the technology evolves, and there is little doubt that AI will develop new functions that change the way academic research and writing are conducted. The overriding point will remain, however: researchers must be critically aware – even sceptical – when responding to AI generated material, and use it in combination with, rather than instead of, our own creativity.

2.4.6 Preparing the final version

At postgraduate level, you should expect to revise your drafts several times before they stabilize into final versions. Leaving a draft piece of work for several days, or even weeks or months, allows you to gain perspective on your work; when you return to the piece, you will almost certainly see where revisions need to be made. Getting feedback on your writing from other people – supervisors, colleagues, friends and those who respond to your presentations in seminars or at conferences – is another way of discovering what does and does not work in your writing. If it doesn't work, no matter how much research it took, material needs to be deleted.

As you finalize your work, you will want to ensure that your grammar and spelling are correct and, most importantly, that all your points are clearly made. You should be prepared to devote considerable time to formatting your references and bibliography correctly. Accurate acknowledgement of sources is crucial for preventing accidental plagiarism. If you are at all unsure about what counts as plagiarism, seek advice from your supervisors and published sources. Two kinds of footnotes or endnotes may be used in your research. As well as those that cite the bibliographic details of the sources you are quoting or discussing (which, in some systems, will appear in parentheses in the main text and not in notes), other notes can be used to give extra information to the reader that, if included in the main text, would disrupt the flow of your argument. However, you should use such discursive notes very sparingly, and only when they present material that is genuinely germane.

In some circumstances, you may need to include one or more appendices at the end of your dissertation. An appendix is not a means of smuggling in material that you have decided has no place in the main body of your work. An appendix usually presents data that readers might need to understand your work, but which would take up too much space in the main text. Examples could include statistical data, the full text of interviews you have conducted and to which you refer in your main text, biographical details of a particular group of authors or readers (called a 'prosopography'), summaries of the plots of largely unknown novels and so on.

The final stages of preparing work for submission include writing a general introduction and conclusion. The introduction normally sets out your research questions, says how you will answer them and explains how original and significant your research is. Your conclusion should summarize your findings, and, ideally, present some new information or discussion that clinches your argument. At last come all the small tasks that seem easy but, together, take a surprising amount of time. These will usually include one or more of the following (depending on the nature of your project and the regulations of your institution):

- preparing a title page
- writing a short abstract of your project
- writing a preface and/or acknowledgements (providing details of those who have helped you in your research, or allowed you to use illustrations or other material)
- compiling a list of illustrations
- preparing a list of abbreviations that you have used frequently
- noting the full word count
- adding a signed statement that the dissertation is entirely your own work and that it has not been previously submitted for any other degree

Finally, you will be ready to submit your work for examination, usually bound (but loosely, so that you can easily add or remove material later) and in two or more copies.

BOX 2.1 EXAMPLE OF A PROPOSAL FOR A UK MASTER'S DISSERTATION IN ENGLISH LITERATURE

1. **Project parameters:**. 20,000 words/80 double-spaced pages, to be completed in one year alongside taught components.
2. **Provisional title:** 'Between Fidelity and Invention: Spin-Off Film Adaptations of Children's Literary Classics'
3. **Aims/rationale:** Almost since the birth of cinema, children's books have been adapted as films: adaptations of *Alice's Adventures in Wonderland* and *The Adventures of Pinocchio* were produced in the 1910s. Neither film companies nor audiences seem to tire of this trend, and in recent years this has led to a new phenomenon: the children's book spin-off movie, or movie franchise. These are films based on children's books, or characters in them, but with new plots and themes especially for the films. They are often prequels or sequels to the children's books from which they draw, and typically expand the books by adding explanatory backstories or inventing the further adventures of the characters. Examples include the *Paddington* films (2014-) based only loosely on Michael Bond's stories; *Cruella* (2021) which develops a character from Dodie Smith's *The Hundred and One Dalmatians* (1956); or *Wonka* (2023) which gives the origin story of a character from Roald Dahl's *Charlie and the Chocolate Factory* (1964). This project aims to explore the history of such adaptations, and ask why they have become so popular now.
4. **Primary sources and availability:** I will confine my study to source books originally published in English, and films made in the United States or United Kingdom. Each film will have been released in 2015 or later. I will focus on a corpus of ten books and the films based on them, and will determine exactly which ten early in my research. Both original source books and films will be easily available in libraries and online.
5. **Existing scholarship:** Much work has been done on the theory and practice of adaptation from literature to film (e.g. Bruhn, 2014; Leitch, 2017) and in the *Journal of Adaptation Studies*. Some of this has focused on the adaptation of children's books, from overviews (Street, 1982; Hermansson, 2019; Meeusen, 2020) to studies of particular texts or franchises like Disney, Harry Potter or *The Hunger Games*, and children's films as a genre are also the subject of several monographs (e.g. Wojcik-Andrews, 2000; Brown, 2017). None has focused specifically on the phenomenon of the children's book 'spin-off' film that I will study, although work has been done on other cinematic 'expanded universes' based on original texts including Jane Austen's and superhero comics. That said, readings of some of my focus films will be useful, such as

analyses of how the Paddington films stretch and bend the original books (Webb, 2018; Smith, 2020).

6. **Research questions:**
   - What is the origin and history of children's book spin-off adaptations?
   - Why has this become such a widespread phenomenon in the early twenty-first century? The economics of filmmaking? Lapses in copyright? Technological changes (such as streaming), changing audiences' tastes or other factors?
   - What kinds of children's books are most likely to generate spin-off films?
   - What relationship do the spin-off films have with the original books? What changes when films expand the worlds of the source texts, for instance in terms of character development, themes as well as visually?
7. **Methodology:** I will start by reading up on the theory of adaptation and the history of children's film. I will read a selection of children's books in conjunction with the spin-off films they have spawned; from these I will select my corpus, choosing book-film dyads that show a full range of approaches to adaptation. I will subject each book and film to close reading while also learning about the economics and practicalities of twenty-first-century cinema, including how films get to be proposed, commissioned and produced.

1. **Chapter outline with provisional word length**

   (1) Introduction. The children's book spin-off film phenomenon and why this should be considered as a distinct and noteworthy genre. An overview of the films which could have been included, and rationale for my corpus. (3,000 words)

   (2) History of film adaptation, especially from children's books, and how the spin-off phenomenon fits into this tradition. (3,000 words)

   (3) Which texts generate spin-offs, and why? (4,000 words)

   (4) Narrative expansion: which aspects of children's texts are developed in spin-off films? (4,000 words)

   (5) How worlds evolve: what changes from text to film? (4,000 words)

   (6) Conclusion (1,000 words)
2. Indicative bibliography

   This section will list primary and secondary texts/films known at this stage. It should be as comprehensive as possible.

BOX 2.2 SAMPLE PROPOSAL FOR A UK DOCTORAL THESIS IN ENGLISH LITERATURE

1. **Project parameters:** 80,000 words/320 double-spaced A4 pages to be completed over three years of full-time study or part-time equivalent (extensions possible).
2. **Provisional title:** 'Representations of enslavement and the transatlantic slave trade in eighteenth-century children's books published in Britain'.
3. **Aims:** To discover whether the debate on enslavement and the transatlantic slave trade featured in works for children in the period before the abolition of the transatlantic slave trade in British colonies in 1807.
4. **Existing scholarship:** Many children's books have been published in the twentieth and twenty-first centuries, especially in the United States, telling the stories of enslaved people. These books have been the subject of some scholarly attention. However, much less has been written about how children's books became part of the debate on the Atlantic slave trade when the debate was taking place in Britian. As my indicative bibliography shows, those few studies mostly consider writing for children alongside writing for adults, or focus on individual children's authors, or examine abolitionist children's literature as published in America in the nineteenth century. My initial research indicates that more primary material exists than has currently been noticed, i.e. children's books from the eighteenth century that represent and consider the subject of transatlantic slave trade and plantation slavery. Some may even be on the pro-slavery side of the debate. It is likely that much useful material will be found in history and geography textbooks designed for children, and that they present a different viewpoint from children's fiction and poetry.
5. **Primary sources and availability:** Eighteenth-century children's books are difficult to obtain, but my university's subscription to the database *Eighteenth-Century Collections Online* (ECCO) will enable me to read much children's literature published in the years 1750–1800, both fiction and non-fiction. ECCO will allow me to identify books containing the words 'slave' and 'slavery', which I will examine individually to isolate children's books. Finding books from the years between 1800 (when ECCO stops) and 1807 (when the transatlantic slave trade was, theoretically, abolished in the British Empire) will be more difficult. Nevertheless, I expect to be able to find more

than fifty relevant titles. For these reasons I propose to limit my study to the years 1775–1800.

6. **Research questions:**
   - To what extent were the transatlantic slave trade and plantation slavery mentioned in children's literature, either directly or indirectly?
   - In what terms was slavery discussed? Were certain motifs and themes common or conventional? Was enslavement presented in factual terms, or did children's writers make their points using fiction? Were illustrations used? Were the brutal realities of slavery openly described, or were they palliated for a child readership?
   - Are enslaved characters ever allowed to speak for themselves and present their experiences of enslavement?
   - Was there more pro- or anti-slavery material in children's books, and were different sides taken by different kinds of authors and publishers? Was slavery discussed in the same terms as characterized the parliamentary debates about the abolition of the slave trade?
   - Were children encouraged to become active in the campaign for or against the slave trade?
7. **Methodology:** I will start by reading about the debate on the transatlantic slave trade in the late eighteenth century, and about children's literature in general in this period. Having read all studies I can find on representations of enslavement in children's literature (in any period), I will begin by searching ECCO for children's books that engage with the debate from the 1770s to 1790s. Whichever books I find, I will read closely, identifying major themes and opinions, and the most common techniques, imagery and motifs that the authors employ to make their points. I will be especially attentive to the nuance of the arguments they present, and any internal tensions within the texts. I will also take note of who wrote and published these books, to see whether pro- or anti-slavery views were generally expressed in work produced by particular groups of people (e.g. religious writers, non-conformists, political reformers). In presenting historical material that could be considered offensive today (both text and images) I will be alert to its effect on readers and offer warnings as appropriate.
8. **Chapter outline, with word lengths**
   1. Introduction: The debate on the slave trade (15,000 words).
   2. Enslavement and the slave trade in children's literature: opponents and defenders (15,000)
   3. How are enslaved people represented and able to articulate their experiences in these texts? (15,000)

4. Making the slavery debate a 'fit subject for children': language, imagery, censorship (15,000)
5. Children as active participants in the debates on slavery and the transatlantic slave trade (15,000)
6. Conclusions (5,000)

9. **Indicative bibliography**
As above, this will be as comprehensive as possible at this stage of the research.

BOX 2.3 FOR AN ITALIAN DOTTORATO DI RICERCA (PHD) THESIS IN ITALIAN LITERATURE (EXAMPLE DEVISED BY ELISA MARAZZI)

1. **Project parameters**: 80,000 words/320 double-spaced A4 pages to be completed over three (or possibly four) years of full-time study (extensions possible).
2. **Provisional title**: 'Representations of ethnic diversity and immigration in books for children published in Italy, 1861-2024'
3. **Aims**: Building on my Laura Magistrale degree in Lettere Moderne and interests in Italian history and education, this doctoral project will establish when ethnic diversity began to be represented in books for children published in Italy; whether this coincided with the introduction of representations of immigration; and when and how these in turn began to be represented. It will situate the Italian experience in the context of the children's books published in other Western European countries. It will conclude by providing an overview of the current representations of immigration in books for children published in twenty-first-century Italy, their reception and their potential to promote diversity and inclusion in Italian society.
4. **Existing scholarship**: The study of children's books and their history has developed as a field only relatively recently in Italy, but scholarly historical accounts have flourished now for two or three decades, including critical studies of different genres and selected publications. However, given the relatively recent emergence of ethnic diversity and immigration as major issues in Italian history and politics, there is little discussion of when and how they began to be represented in children's books. Colonial fiction for children published in the early twentieth century may have included the first books with accounts of encounters between Italian children and children/adults from different ethnic backgrounds, but as my indicative bibliography shows, such literature has so far been studied only from a political point

of view (how it contributed to and portrayed Italy's short-lived and controversial colonial efforts). However, after the end of the Second World War and consequent decolonialization, and in contrast with some other Western European countries, questions of ethnic diversity were once again largely absent from Italian society. My initial research suggests that even in the 1980s and 1990s, when Italian publishers began to invest consistently in children's books, when society began to recognize their value, and when immigration from abroad increased, ethnic diversity appeared only in a few titles translated from English. An in-depth study of the titles published and a close reading of selected works will enable me to provide the first account of how Italian children's books have included, described and promoted immigration narratives and ethnic integration. This research will be carried out with an awareness of the social and political context that has led to a rapid and turbulent increase in the ethnic diversity of Italian society.

5. **Primary sources and availability**: My corpus (tentatively around 150 books) will be built through advanced research in the national online public access catalogue (OPAC SBN), using a carefully designed set of keywords. These keywords will also be used to search the catalogues of historical libraries specializing in children's literature, for example, the historical library of the Fondazione Mondadori for titles published from the 1980s onwards; the Fondazione Tancredi di Barolo and the Fondazione Colonnetti in Turin, and the Cotsen Children's Library (Princeton, United States) for earlier children's books – as well as current publishers' catalogues. This will allow me to build up a corpus of texts, which may not be complete, since children's books are less well preserved, but which (thanks to the special collections mentioned) will probably be representative of overall production. Such a corpus will be the subject of close reading. For some earlier cases, digitized editions may be available, and for contemporary cases, digital editions should be accessible: this will also allow me to search for keywords related to race and immigration in the texts. Paratextual elements of the books in the corpus, such as illustrations, covers and series information, will also be subject to close scrutiny.
6. **Research questions**:
    - What does 'ethnic diversity' mean in the context of Italian children's books, and how will this thesis use and interrogate this concept?
    - When did representations of ethnic diversity first appear in children's books published in Italy? How does this compare with other Western European countries?

- Do these representations of diversity appear in original texts or in translations? If in translations, where are the source texts from? Is there a time lag between the original publication and the translation into Italian?
- What is the impact of the colonial efforts of the early twentieth century on the presence in books of characters from ethnic backgrounds other than Italian?
- What impact did the beginning of immigration to Italy in the late twentieth century have on ethnic diversity in children's books? When did the first stories about immigration appear in children's books? Are these books original texts or translations? If they are translations, where do the original texts come from? Is there a time lag between the original publication and the translation into Italian?
- What terms and tropes are used to describe and present ethnic diversity and immigration? Are there recurring themes and narratives? To what extent are these uniquely Italian?
- How do illustrations, covers and other paratextual elements contribute to the representation of ethnic diversity and immigration?
- Are there differences between the choices made by commercial publishers and books published through charitable sector projects (in terms of if, when and how they deal with the representation of diversity and immigration)?
- Are there variations over time as governments change their stance on immigration and integration?
- Is it possible to detect an interest of some authors/translators/publishers in promoting inclusion? Can we assess the results of such efforts?

7. **Methodology**: I will begin by reading about the history of Italian colonialism; international immigration to Italy; the social and ethnic composition of society; historical and critical accounts of children's literature. This will include reading about other national contexts, so as to understand how scholars have dealt with similar issues in different contexts, and in my first year, I will apply to join an international programme to enable me to study abroad for six months under the supervision of a local, recognized, scholar in the field. Whether or not my application for an international placement is successful, I will spend my first year defining my corpus, considering factors such as the target age of readers, whether to include picturebooks, inclusion of books produced in the public sector, etc. I will then outline a set of keywords that I will use to search online catalogues and databases for Italian children's books that deal with ethnic diversity and immigration. I will read the books I find closely, identifying the main themes and the most common

techniques, images and motifs used by the authors. I will also pay attention to the material features of the books, to see how paratexts contribute to the ideas and perspectives the authors are promoting. I will also note who wrote and published these books; whether they were originals or translations; size of print runs, and different editions and sales figures, if available. This will allow me to see whether representations of diversity and immigration and their impact on children's lives have been promoted by particular groups (e.g. radical authors and/or publishers, charities and foundations and so on) and which books seem to be more successful in the book trade. I will also try to find reviews of the books in the general and specialized media, as well as information on their use in schools, acquisition by libraries, presence at literary festivals and other forms of distribution. All this will contribute to a full understanding of the reception of these books, and their potential to promote inclusion in contemporary and future societies.

8. **Chapter outline, with word lengths**
    1. Introduction: state of the art; methodology; outline of the work; international contexts and comparisons (10,000 words)
    2. Occurrence and perception of ethnic diversity in the history of the Italian state (15,000 words)
    3. First encounters with 'the other' in books for children in the age of Italian Imperialism (10,000 words)
    4. Narrating immigration in books for children published in Italy in the twentieth and twenty-first centuries: stories, themes, paratexts (20,000 words)
    5. Authors, translators, publishers (15,000 words)
    6. Assessing the reception of twenty-first-century books for children dealing with immigration and ethnic diversity (sales, reviews, debate, acquisition by libraries, adoptions in schools) (10,000 words)
    7. Appendix: bibliographic data of the books included in the corpus (chronological list with indexes); illustrations
9. **Bibliography**

2.5. FURTHER READING AND RESOURCES

Bradford, C. (2007), *Unsettling Narratives: Postcolonial Readings of Children's Literature*, Waterloo, ON: Wilfrid Laurier University Press.

Hunt, P. (1991), *Criticism, Theory and Children's Literature*, Oxford: Blackwell.

Lathey, G. (2015), *Translating Children's Literature*, London: Routledge.

Literature Online: https://about.proquest.com/en/products-services/literature_online/.

MLA International Bibliography: https://www.ebsco.com/products/research-databases/mla-international-bibliography-full-text.

Moorhouse, B., M. Yeo, and Y. Wan (2023), 'Generative AI Tools and Assessment: Guidelines of the World's Top-ranking Universities', *Computers and Education*, 5: 1–10. https://doi.org/10.1016/j.caeo.2023.100151.

3

Ethics and children's literature studies, edited by Tyler Bickford and Emily Murphy

Introduction by Emily Murphy

Children's literature studies is rapidly expanding in new and exciting directions. As we outline in the introduction to this volume, children and young people (CYP) is a broad category that captures the audience for children's literature. As scholars and practitioners with a stake in children's literature work to engage CYP communities, it becomes necessary to think more about the ethics involved when working with a group of individuals that is considered more vulnerable and in need of protection. 'Protection' usually means considering a child's right to privacy, which despite variations in institutional policies around ethics, is one area where there is broadly a consensus across nations. This is reflected in the fact that CYP communities have this basic right protected by the Convention on the Rights of the Child, which to date has been ratified by 196 countries.

So what do we mean by ethics? This chapter outlines different ethical considerations that are involved when it comes to working with CYP. While many of the contributions in this section reflect the more child-centred focus within children's literature studies, each contributor attends to the importance of taking the adult-child relationship seriously when engaging with CYP communities. For some, this will be a challenge that they face every day in their work within children's literature studies, including those working in museums and archives where children are gaining more access and power to help shape these spaces. For those conducting research with CYP communities, it might mean engaging in rigorous ethical review processes or spending long periods of times (often years) building a relationship with the institutions where young people spend much of their time, be it schools, nurseries or community centres. However, even for those not working directly with CYP communities, there remain important ethical questions about the role of researchers and practitioners and their responsibilities when it comes to working with children's books and materials developed for children and young people. In preparing yourself for these forms of ethical inquiry, it is therefore important to build on earlier questions about your identity ('What kind of researcher am I?') as a researcher to include how you wish to practice your research ('How will I carry out my research?'). While the two questions are related, they are not one and the same.

How will I carry out my research?

At some point, you will need to grapple with the question of how you wish to carry out your research, whether you find yourself as the principal investigator on a research project or leading a new outreach campaign for an institution in the heritage sector. Here, we use 'research' inclusively to encompass a broad range of work that includes CYP communities, including the type of engagement work that may be more common within sectors outside of academia with a focus on children's literature studies. Even outside of academia, there are still strict protocols and guidance for engaging with children and young people, and so these questions remain relevant. Some of the questions you may ask yourself when embarking for the first time on a project that actively engages children and young people are:

- What do I know about the children and young people in the communities I plan to engage or work with?
- Who are the gatekeepers (or those with legal responsibility) of CYP in these communities? How can I build a relationship with these individuals as well?
- How will I balance my aims as a researcher and the aims of the CYP I work with? Am I willing to be flexible on the outcomes of the project? (This may depend on how your work is being funded. It's always best to build in flexibility to funding bids to reflect your ethos as a researcher, especially if you must report back on your findings or publish public documents based on your research.)

This list is by no means exhaustive. Doing ethically responsible research with CYP communities is complex, and increasingly so as many scholars within children's literature studies work across disciplines or take up new research approaches that challenge previous notions of what it means to 'do' children's literature studies. It is becoming more common to engage directly with children and young people when talking about children's literature, which means that considering the ethical questions that arise from research within the field is essential.

3.1 Building trust with CYP communities by Ani Rosa Almario and Gabriela Lee

Many research questions and projects benefit directly from interventions or opportunities to have children and young people contribute directly. This may come in the form of interviews, surveys, directed or undirected activities or feedback sessions. However, since CYP communities are among some of the more vulnerable groups in society, it is crucial that researchers are conscious of the ethical dimension of their work when it comes to approaching them and building rapport. Gaining the trust of the CYP we want to work with is an important first step in the process.

Trust can be loosely defined as a bi-directional relationship between two or more individuals in which there is mutual affinity and respect, such that each person has the other's best interest at heart. However, in child-adult relationships, there is an imbalance because adults often occupy positions of control over children. This hierarchy of control may negatively impact how children learn to trust adults, especially if they experienced abuse or neglect from the adults around them.

Building trust with CYP communities relies on how we approach them as individuals. According to Griffith and Johnson, there are four approaches to building trust with CYP. They are:

1. Respect
2. Rapport
3. Consistency
4. Role-playing

Respecting young people is the first step in establishing a connection of trust. This may take the form of acknowledging them as individuals by, for example, learning their names and preferred pronouns, or showing vulnerability in front of them by sharing an authentic and honest experience that models showing trust. Creating rapport is the next step, and it usually involves finding activities or actions that minimize the hierarchical gap between adults and young people. Playing games or partaking in youth-led activities are examples of ways in which rapport can be built. Respect and rapport are key to establishing consistency in relationships with young people. Consistency can include being present at regular intervals, avoiding appearances of favouritism by interacting with each person equally and being available to their questions. Finally, role-playing involves taking on a specific and nuanced role as an adult in their lives

– an adult who is not necessarily related or in a professional role. In a way, this also means modelling what a positive and safe interaction with an adult might look like, especially if the CYP communities you intend to approach have experienced trauma, abuse or neglect.

3.2 Case study: Raya School

After the home, the school is the most significant place for trust-building between adults and CYP. In the Raya School, a progressive school in the Philippines, adults who work with the students utilize all four of Griffith and Johnson's approaches to building trust to guide them through their everyday challenges and issues.

After the children came back from the prolonged Covid-19 lockdown, the adults in the school noticed the prevalence of gender-related issues. These issues emerged mostly during middle school, a time when many young people are grappling with their identities and finding the most affirmation from their peers. Some may identify with the gender they were not assigned at birth, while others venture outside the gender binary, wish to go unlabelled, or assert the use of personal pronouns that do not correspond with the gender assigned at birth. The potentially difficult process of coming out in school or at home may be done more painlessly with the guidance of a trusted adult.

For the students to feel comfortable opening up about their gender-related issues with adults such as researchers, it is necessary for these adults to show them respect: using their preferred pronouns and/or new names and also taking the time to listen to them when they share stories about their everyday lives. Taking the time to listen to them and having real conversations also builds rapport. In guided conversation, researchers need to pick up on the students' interests – hobbies, pets, favourite online activities and games and close friends. Initial conversations are usually centred around these interests, but once the connection and trust become more established, they grow deeper.

Conversations can then begin to tackle family issues, peer-related issues and issues around gender and identity.

For instance, some students may reveal sensitive information, such as the difficulty of coming out to their families. Students who feel that most people in school are accepting of their new gender identity may sometimes fear interactions with members of the school community who are not as inclusive. This is where consistency and role-playing come in. As the adult researcher, one has consistently to show acceptance and support to students facing gender-related challenges. They also have to be accessible to these students, as some may have episodes of mental breakdown or depression. This can be challenging for the adults since it may necessitate being available after work hours, in online spaces or even during weekends. For many of these students, their teachers and guidance counsellors take on the role of trusted adults, helping students understand the complex feelings and reactions that come with their new gender identities. However, when conducting research on gender-related topics, a researcher might find out about students' issues before their parents. One must, therefore, learn how to be careful about navigating family relationships: not overstepping boundaries, respecting the feelings and wishes of students and maintaining the trust and partnership with parents. Creating a trustworthy bond with CYP provides them with the opportunity to be actively involved in shaping knowledge about themselves and building communities that can influence their lives in the present and the future.

3.3 Gaining ethical permission for sensitive projects by Tyler Bickford

While most research in children's literature studies focuses on existing texts or archives, research directly involving CYP can require additional procedures for securing ethics approvals from the institutions we work in. Requirements vary between countries and across institutions (and funding agencies may have their own policies), and around the world research ethics policies are transforming rapidly as national and regional research and education sectors expand and change. In general, it is common for research involving 'human subjects' to meet certain standards and to receive formal approval from an institutional ethics board. While the specific processes and language may vary, the underlying principles and concepts are similar, especially minimizing risks to participants and ensuring that participants give 'informed consent'.

The ethics approval process is important: it gets us thinking carefully about our research in productive ways, and it helps establish us as participants in a broader interdisciplinary community of researchers. But it can also present real challenges. In particular, the process can be long and complicated and may create significant delays. This can be especially challenging for early career researchers with inflexible deadlines set by their degree programme or terms of employment (e.g., tenure policies). Additionally, many institutions design their ethics procedures around biomedical research; these models do not always fit well with work in children's literature and childhood studies.

What is 'human subjects research'?

Almost any research that involves acquiring and analysing information from living individuals (including observations, interviews, surveys and experiments) is considered human subjects research and may require some form of ethics review. Public information that already exists, such as published texts, datasets from other researchers or documents in archives, is not normally considered human subjects research. Therefore, while such methods may still raise sensitive ethical considerations, they frequently do not require formal ethics approval. Information posted on social media can be a grey area, and different institutions may treat it differently. While uncommon, some institutions may even require ethics approval for every research project, regardless of the involvement of human subjects. It is important to be familiar with the specific policies and requirements at your institution.

Risks and benefits

Unlike biomedical research, which can involve collecting tissue or giving new drugs, most research in the humanities poses minimal risks to participants, which often allows for a streamlined approval process. But because CYP are generally considered a vulnerable population, even minimal risk research with young subjects (or research that involves sensitive topics such as self-harm or drug use) is still likely to require a robust approval process. Since CYP who participate in humanities research are not likely to be at risk of physical harm, the primary risks ethics reviewers are likely to identify are to their privacy or reputation and potential emotional distress. This means that it is common for reviewers to require that researchers fully anonymize child participants' identities. For many projects this is fine, but in some cases it conflicts with our ethical obligation to give credit to our interlocutors and to acknowledge their intellectual contributions. Anonymizing participants risks harming them by using their ideas or contributions without attribution when their reputation or self-esteem may benefit from such attribution. For ethics boards that are often focused on biomedical research, such risks and benefits can be unfamiliar, and reviewers can be strongly inclined to prioritize the better-established risks of privacy or reputational damage. This varies by institution, but in some cases it can create serious challenges for certain approaches to participatory research with CYP (see Section 3.5). If acknowledging your research participants is a priority for you, you may need to undertake additional advocacy or seek support from mentors or colleagues to gain approval.

Informed consent

A basic principle of research ethics is that participants freely choose to participate. This means that they must be fully informed of the potential risks and benefits of their participation, and that they can choose to stop participating at any time. Research involving CYP adds a layer of complexity because this group is commonly understood (especially by legalistic bureaucracies) to lack the full ability to give their consent. Ethics approval boards sometimes require a two-step process, in which CYP are asked to 'assent', and their parents or guardians are asked to formally 'consent'. For children's literature and childhood studies researchers, this limitation on CYP's own decision-making can be problematic, but it reflects deeply established legal and cultural norms in most Western countries that can rarely be contested. This process can in fact be useful for ensuring that important caregivers are informed and on board and as a way of talking with CYP about the project's aims and their own priorities and hopes for it. Ethical approval, then, can help encourage young research participants to think about your research and how they might contribute as partners as much as subjects.

Conclusion

If you are thinking about doing research with CYP, you need to start thinking about the ethics of your project and the ethics approval process as early as possible. As the other sections of this chapter make clear, ethical questions have a direct bearing on our theories, methods and topics. The formal ethics approval process is also something that connects us to colleagues working in a wide range of other disciplines, and it can both validate your research to such audiences and help build connections with new fields and collaborators. But ethics approval also adds another layer to the research process, and it is easy to get caught by surprise by your institution's requirements. Ask colleagues or mentors about your institution's ethics review process and start orienting yourself right away. Many institutions offer regular ethics approval trainings, where you can learn much about the process and about research that colleagues in other fields are doing. Thinking systematically about risks, benefits and informed consent is often very generative. Ethics issues are never separate from research design; the earlier you start thinking about your own ethical values and priorities, the better prepared you will be to complete a sometimes complex approval process, and even more importantly, the more rigorous and insightful your research will be.

3.4 Participatory research by Justyna Deszcz-Tryhubczak

Participatory research or children's and young people's research involves children as researchers in their own right in all stages of the research process – from identifying research needs and designing methods, through data analysis, to the dissemination of results. It is often intended as not just a means of gaining data about children's lives, but also of facilitating children's use of their findings to shape policies regarding matters that matter to them. Research *with*, and just not *about*, children and young people, is well established in childhood studies and reflected in its intensifying commitment to a decolonization of childhood research and practice. This is not only 'in the conventional sense of confronting Western civilizing constructions of childhood', but also as a means to challenge adultist knowledge production about children and young people reflecting prejudices against their capabilities (Cheney, 2018: 91). It is also hoped that participatory research with children will lead to epistemic diversity that will make children's and young people's knowledge legitimate in the eyes of researchers, policymakers, educators and in society in general.

Children's participation in research has also become important in children's literature studies, a field traditionally focused on adult discussions of texts addressed to child audiences. Recent projects relying on research with children and young people usually focus on their cultural activities in the past, the current rise of young authors and reviewers, and youth activism inspired by children's culture (Deszcz-Tryhubczak, 2024). While such ventures are usually limited in scope and representation, they are important as situated research responding to the needs of specific intergenerational cross-expertise communities, and because they are potentially capable of transforming these communities for the benefit of all generations. Children's literature and culture are important factors in these transformations.

Children's and young people's protagonism in research has given rise to a fascinating interdisciplinary debate urging scholars to review both the ethical protocols of their institutions and their own theoretical assumptions and practices aimed at ensuring child participants' welfare, protecting their rights, dignity and autonomy in research, and maintaining individual and institutional accountability (see e.g. Hanson and Spyrou; Loveridge et al., 2023). This diligence is of utmost importance in light of the increasing commitment across disciplinary fields to counteract epistemic extractivism and datafication of childhood that results from the neo-liberal pressure for efficient data collection and quick outputs (Spyrou, 2023). A significant part of this commitment is a growing emphasis on the relational nature of research as a collective practice based on respect, care, reciprocity and responsibility. Similar explorations are also gaining traction in children's literature and culture scholarship, meaning that a reflective approach to ethics of participatory research with children and young people should also emerge in our field.

The following example from my participatory research with children illustrates the intricacies of pursuing relational ethics in situ. Inspired by our earlier collaborations with child researchers in two interrelated projects (Chawar et al., 2018; Deszcz-Tryhubczak et al., 2019), my colleague Mateusz Marecki and I invited the children from those projects to co-author two peer-reviewed publications with us and their teacher (also involved in both projects). These documented the results of our joint research and recognized the children's scholarly work and research ownership. Our intergenerational team needed to address three major ethical issues. Firstly, we had to consider potential risks and harms involved in the children's publishing both articles under their own names. The young participants and their parents were aware of the long duration of scholarly publications. Moreover, both projects emphasized children's right to shape school reading lists and questioned the current political ideologies in Poland that resulted, among others, in fully centralized decisions concerning the curriculum, with no room for teachers' and students' choices. We were therefore afraid that the subversive contents of the publications could somehow endanger our young co-authors, even if Poland is a free country and the publications were to appear in English.

We explained our choice of international journals to the child participants, who agreed with us and were keen to share their experiences and findings in Poland and elsewhere. Their parents and the teacher supported their decision. We also needed to determine the form of the articles as we wanted to avoid overburdening the children by expecting them to learn standards of academic writing. By structuring the articles as polyvocal narratives, with each section specifying the names of its authors and written in their own style, we hoped to convey relational understandings emerging from our projects and foreground the young people's insider perspectives. Recognizing the children's ownership of their research, we also required the journals' editors to list their names as co-authors. Importantly, while in our case acknowledging their authorship was an obvious ethical commitment, we realized that this may not be the best course of action when the research focus is sensitive. Including real names or pseudonyms should always be discussed with the child participants and their parents or carers. Also, in our case, there were no institutional ethics approval concerns raised, but other institutions may require additional steps for identifying child research participants. To summarize, our joint articles could not have been written without our situated ethical considerations and a sense of reciprocity and accountability, which we shared with all the participants (see Deszcz-Tryhubczak and Marecki, 2021).

The above example of ethical issues involved in children's participation in research merits a more general perspective: we may think of research with children and young people not just in terms of collecting data as our primary goal but also as an ethical intervention in current social and political predicaments experienced by children and adults (Spyrou). These projects constituted our shared attempt at questioning the status quo by enabling the emergence of an intergenerational collective committed to have a say in shaping the curriculum. I suggest that it is our ongoing ethical responsibility as scholars to identify contexts and practices related to children's literature and culture that enable our research to respond to the needs of local communities. In this way, we may, to some extent, transform these communities through fostering collaborations for the benefit of all generations.

3.5 The ethics behind archival research by Devika Mehra

This section briefly overviews ethical issues that may arise when planning and conducting archival research (see Chapter 5). Archives and special collections in libraries and museums are part of a complex information system that includes physical collections and digital archives. Several digitization efforts worldwide have been transforming vast archival collections into digital archives in recent years, raising further ethical concerns. Archival materials, including books, manuscripts and proofs, unpublished works, correspondence, illustrations, photographs, postcards, toys, games and clothes, often contain Personally Identifiable Information (PII), are bound by copyright and permissions, and usually have limitations placed by donor/s or licensing terms in the case of digital collections. Understanding the ethical concerns involved in how researchers access and use these archives to exchange and disseminate information to various audiences is essential. Moreover, in the case of children's literature studies, there are further ethical issues surrounding original works or artefacts produced by CYP. It raises several questions about navigating permissions and handling this material responsibly (see also Section 3.3).

Having identified the research topic and question, you will want to consider any ethical questions related to it or the types of archival materials you plan to consult. You will want to deal with basic permissions, copyrights and licences, and be aware of any restrictions placed on the archives. You will have to acquire the required permissions for any data publicly released as part of scholarly publication, presentation, exhibition or toolkit after completion of the project. In some cases, the donor may have placed limitations, or they may be unaware of all the information included in the collection, or it may consist of PII. For instance, correspondence often contains multiple authors, including those of children and young people, and the correspondents whose letters have been archived may not always be aware of their presence in a special collection of children's literature. This contains sensitive information, including PII, such as names, addresses, schools and email addresses, and other indirect identifying information, such as demographic features, gender, race, nationality and geographic location data. In rare instances, an author may have gained written permission before donating their personal letters (see Box 3.1), but these types of examples are few and far between. Therefore, the responsibility lies with you as the researcher when determining how to handle sensitive personal information. You should ensure privacy and confidentiality at all stages of your research and it is best practice to avoid any identifying information in any subsequent research outputs.

BOX 3.1 BEVERLEY NAIDOO: GAINING ETHICAL PERMISSION FROM CYP

BEVERLEY NAIDOO IS AN AWARD-WINNING British children's author. Best known for her depiction of apartheid in South Africa, the author has received the prestigious Carnegie Award for her book *The Other Side of Truth*, among other accolades. Having previously worked as an educator, Naidoo placed great emphasis on working closely with children as she developed her stories, a practice that is reflected in her archives in Seven Stories, the National Centre for Children's Books. A closer look at one of the letters she received from a child demonstrates the ethical issues that may arise when conducting archival research. In a letter dated 13 June 1990, Naidoo writes, 'Three years ago you wrote me a wonderful letter after you had read my book "Journey to Jo'burg". In my reply I am sure I must have said how good it was to receive such a thoughtful letter which asked so many important questions'. Naidoo goes on to relate how she 'often quoted anonymously' from this child's letter 'to show the sort of questions a young person is capable of asking'; in this letter she formally requests permission to publish an excerpt for use in a radio programme. As the producers of the programme had requested that the child's name be revealed as the author of the letter, Naidoo chose to gain her formal consent, including a copy of the original as a reminder of what she has been sent.

The response to Naidoo is equally revealing. The girl, Azra, says, 'I was surprised to hear from you, after such a long time . . . I'm really pleased to know that my letter ~~to you~~ was helpful to you. Now after three years, I've read it again, it was hard for me to believe it was me that wrote the letter. I don't think I do stuff like that anymore. Anyway I would be happy for you to use my letter' ('Letter to Naidoo', 25 June, 1990). The response to Naidoo's request for the girl's consent to quote her letter in a public forum reveals some of the grey areas of permissions in the archive. While the legal requirements to more strictly regulate the use of PII (Personal Identifiable Information) in the UK and Europe (known as General Data Protection Regulation) did not take effect until 2018, Naidoo recognized that the shift from informally sharing excerpts from a personal letter to her, especially when anonymized, is not the same as sharing these excerpts to a wider audience while also revealing the letter writer's name. While Azra was happy to have her original letter quoted, she was given the agency to decide this for herself and was also able to flag to Naidoo that her surname had changed, therefore ensuring her correct name was used when her work was shared on the radio programme. The fact that Azra did not remember the contents of the letter, and even felt she had changed quite a bit since writing those words, also leaves space for the author to reflect on how to contextualize the original letter and its contents.

Within archives and special collections, working directly with the author or creator of an archival record is a form of 'participatory practice' that acknowledges the 'right to the record' of multiple stakeholders. In this case, while Naidoo is the named person of the collection where Azra's letter resides, it is ultimately the girl (an adult by now) who maintains ownership of this particular record. While no legal requirements would bind a researcher to gaining further permission to reprint this letter in a publication, best practice is to gain this permission or to anonymize its contents if that is not possible. In most cases it is impossible to track down the authors of letters from CYP, particularly when they are from many years ago, meaning it is up to researchers to determine what PII it is reasonable to reveal. In some cases, the donor may be the author of the personal item (a letter or school exercise book) and have donated to a collection that makes records public, therefore recognizing the possibility that their work will be shared publicly in the future.

Another vital scenario is if you discover unpublished works and want to use them in your research outputs for public use. You have an ethical responsibility to treat this sensitively, secure the necessary permissions, and use this information after clarifying any restrictions or limitations that the donors may have placed on sharing such information from the collections. Even if the author or creator of these materials is no longer living, the right to give permission to make these materials public usually lies with their living relatives. Moreover, there are generally other individuals with a right to these records, including the authors of fan mail, such as young children. While there are many grey areas surrounding ethical permission to use such materials, you need to remember that gaining ethical permission will not be as simple as writing to the special collection or archive where you conducted your research. Keeping track of who has the right to give permission at the point of your visit will help save you time later when you wish to publish your work. You could consult the library staff, the archivists and the collections manager to navigate this.

At this early stage, it is useful to consult with your institution to see if any formal ethics procedure may be required (see Section 3.3). While archival research is not held to the same strict ethical procedures as research directly involving children, the emergence of more interdisciplinary work in the field means that many projects with an archival research component cross into areas that will require some form of ethical approval. As an example, if conducting outreach work with children that involves the production of original materials, you will need to consider any additional approval or safeguarding measures, even if your topic does not appear to be of a sensitive nature. Additional measures to protect children and their identities may be necessary even when working in archives. Often, it requires careful consideration of questions of power imbalances and privacy. This is especially true when working in archives that are not designated special collections, such as in schools where many items are not intended for public display. While you may find similar items as those within special collections of children's literature, the location of these materials in an educational setting for CYP means that a greater awareness of the rights of the owners of these archival records must be respected.

As an example of these ethical issues, I share a case study of one of my projects where I investigated racial diversity, prize culture and the role of young people. For this research, I consulted Black British children's literature archives (mainly archives of Grace Hallworth, Grace Nichols, Valerie Bloom and John Agard) held at Seven Stories, the National Centre for Children's Books. Ethical considerations arose as much of the material (including unpublished works, correspondence (print and born-digital), letters, artwork, poetry from schoolchildren and photographs) I was working with concerned living authors. Moreover, as this collection references race, migration and discrimination, sensitivity to the context in which these materials were produced was important, especially when using this material for knowledge-production activities for the public. Such sensitivity issues are essential when dealing with archival material important to historically minoritized communities.

As part of my project, I co-designed learning and teaching resources for schools in collaboration with Seven Stories. For this, I had to focus on material related specifically to Windrush, referring to the period of immigration from the Caribbean to the UK marked by the arrival of the HMT Empire Windrush in Tilbury, Essex in 1948, and understanding race and racism in children's books. These critical thinking toolkits, specifically developed using Black British children's literature archives, co-created new approaches to studying historical events such as the Windrush and using archives to experiment with alternative modes of knowledge co-production to be used within educational settings. In designing these toolkits, we had to be careful about sensitivity and privacy issues, especially when using some of the material, such as unpublished poems and children's letters to authors discovered during archival research. For example, with the help of the Seven Stories team, we gained permission from the authors to use some unpublished poems by John Agard from this collection. We had to be mindful of maintaining the data privacy of school children whose letters were part of this collection. Care was taken to ensure no PII or sensitive information was disclosed at any project stage.

The turn towards digital technology has impacted the ethical considerations related to archival practice and research, especially by widening access at the global level. On the one hand, digital interventions are increasing the accessibility of this information system, which can be consumed and circulated in various contexts. On the other hand, digitized archives may be without proper contextualization, especially when it concerns culturally sensitive materials, providing only partial information, or using outdated language that may further increase racial and other stereotypes. For instance, the Endangered Archives programme enables researchers to access digitized archives of collections held in remote places. Researchers can view digitized records of early twentieth-century children's periodicals from Bengal, access the metadata and understand the language used to contextualize such records. Digitization of archives opens up ethical questions of representation, biases, and the harm caused by improper metadata and creates a space for researchers to consider social justice and inclusion along with ethical concerns. Likewise, there are emerging ethical considerations in the case of born-digital records related to data protection, PII, copyright and sensitivity issues. You need to develop an ethics of care and sensitivity (Odumosu, 2020), especially when dealing with Indigenous collections and colonial archives. Apart from paying attention to what archival materials you access and consult, you need to be aware of how the entire knowledge organization system and its metadata are constructed.

3.6 Case study: Sharing stories from diverse communities by Nithya Sivashankar

I am a South Asian and a non-resident scholar in the United States, who researches not only South Asian and diasporic children's literature, but also refugee and displacement narratives from the Middle East. I have researched and written about picturebooks set in African countries, and those portraying indigenous and diasporic foods. While some of the research that I have done overlaps with my positionality, the rest of it has made me question the ethical implications of a cultural 'outsider' like me engaging in research about topics for which I do not have lived experience and writing about stories and characters with whom I do not share positionalities. I have struggled with evaluating stories based on standard definitions of accuracy and authenticity, wondering about my own cultural qualifications to engage in such judgement. When a student or scholar of children's literature looks up definitions of cultural accuracy or those of a cultural insider/outsider, they are likely to come upon the works of Rudine Sims Bishop, Michelle H. Martin, Junko Yokota, Weimin Mo, Wenju Shen, Dana L. Fox and Kathy G. Short. A review of their research on cultural accuracy and authenticity reveals that defining these terms is a complex endeavour. Moreover, as my colleagues and I state elsewhere, 'in an increasingly global and transnational world, in which most cultural groups do not have clearly defined borders, it is necessary to complicate and reframe our understanding of cultural authenticity beyond the outsider/insider binary' (Sivashankar *et.al.*, 2020: 482).

As scholars, it becomes our responsibility to engage in responsible and ethical engagement practices in order to research and write about books that a) fall outside the purview of our cultural and lived experiences and b) are written and illustrated by creators who do not share cultural positionalities with the characters that they are writing about. Over the course of my research on Anglo-American picturebooks about Arab refugees, I noticed that nearly 90 per cent of the narratives published on this topic until 2020 were written and illustrated by non-Arab creators. It led me to question how to write responsibly about representations of refugees as a non-refugee academic studying the works of authors and illustrators who were neither refugees nor Arab. It also led me to question the larger ethical implications of such a piece of writing. With these questions in mind, when I investigated their content using the framework of rhetorical narratology, I discovered narrative ethics, which stresses four important aspects involved in the ethical consideration of texts.

James Phelan points out that 'narratives themselves implicitly or explicitly ask the question, 'How should one think, judge, and act – as author, narrator, character, or audience – for the greater good?' (2014: 531). He notes that inquiring into narrative ethics would mean engaging with one or more of the following: (1) 'Ethics of the told', which deals with the characters' actions in the narrative, the conflicts they encounter, and the ethical decisions that they choose to make; (2) 'Ethics of the telling', which focuses on the ethical dimensions of the discourse in the narrative and how those, in turn, bear on the relationship between the implied authors, narrators, narratees and implied readers; (3) 'Ethics of writing/producing', which in Phelan's words, concerns itself with 'text-external matters involving actual authors. . . or other constructing agents' and their ethical obligations and implications, and (4) 'Ethics of reading/reception', which centralizes the actual audiences and 'the consequences of their engagements with narratives' (531–32).

Additionally, I found the narrative-ethics lens valuable for exploring picturebooks about war, immigration and forced displacement because, as readers (especially those of us who are not migrants or refugees), it is our ethical responsibility to participate conscientiously in the stories of those who are different from us. While as scholars we are inclined to invest in the ethics of characters' choices and decisions, it is important also to consider the ethics of the storytelling process, the ethics of publication, the agents involved in the production of these narratives, and the ethics of audiences' engagement with the narratives. It is essential that we, as responsible researchers, question and investigate the ethics involved in the writing, publication, marketing and reception of the texts, alongside examining the narratives themselves.

Children's literature has been and is being read, appreciated, critiqued and taught for its aesthetic and moral values across the world. It is impossible to account for morality without including ethics in the equation. As readers and scholars of children's literature, it is essential for us to keep in mind that these narratives written for a young audience serve as ideological vehicles that introduce and shape sociocultural opinions and values to children. Additionally, it is also important for us to recognize our social positioning as well as that of our students and children in order to reflect critically on how our positioning affects us as readers and critics of narratives. Narrative ethics is a useful framework for opening up 'the multi-layered intersections of narrative [and its ideological] and moral values' (Phelan: 532). Thus, I propose that scholars and students of children's literature adopt this approach to take more players and their ethical commitments into the reading and evaluation experience. It suggests that we need to think more critically about our own positionalities as readers, in addition to investigating the text and understanding the contexts of publication and reception of the narrative.

3.7 Conclusion by Emily Murphy

While it is impossible to discuss all the ethical issues that may arise when conducting research in children's literature studies, this chapter provides examples that can help frame critical self-reflection on your research practice. We began by asking, 'How will I carry out my research?' as a way of framing how to begin this process. As the contributors to this section underscore, to answer this question it is imperative both to navigate practical requirements for projects that engage with CYP communities and to consider methodological practices that help resolve more ethically dubious forms of inquiry. Even when it comes to something as mundane as completing citations for your references, you may have to take steps to protect the identities of children and young people in a way that is at odds with reference style conventions. And, just as not all CYP communities are the same, the way you approach each new research or engagement project will differ. As you begin developing an ethically responsible research method, you may wish to refine the questions that we opened with at the beginning of this chapter, considering the following:

- What have I learned from my previous work with CYP communities? Are there any elements of my current research practice that are at odds with my philosophical beliefs about the best way to engage with members of these communities?
- What resources do I need to become more ethical in my approach with CYP communities? (This could involve additional training from practitioners experienced in working with children and young people.)
- How will I communicate the importance of the ethical steps I am taking in working with CYP communities to funding bodies, both internal and external, so that I can continue to have the financial support needed to create long-lasting and meaningful relationships with children and young people?
- Are there any areas where I feel action is needed in order to change current practices for engaging with CYP communities? (This could be through discussion with colleagues in children's literature studies or the internal ethical committees that review and grant approval for proposed research activity).

As with the previous list, these questions are not exhaustive and you will need to think carefully about the extent to which you wish to follow established rules and guidance for ethically engaging with CYP communities and how much your research will be driven by discovery, including through the development of new methodologies or practices for working with those in these communities. Whatever you choose, by taking time to reflect on your identity as a researcher, you will already be engaging in the necessary steps to be more conscious about the ethics involved in working with children and young people.

3.8 FURTHER READING AND RESOURCES

Participatory Research

Eckhoff, A., ed. (2019), *Participatory Research with Young Children*, Cham: Springer. https://doi.org/10.1007/978-3-030-19365-2.

Groundwater-Smith, S., S. Dockett, and D. Bottrell, eds (2015), *Participatory Research with Children and Young People*, London: SAGE. https://doi.org/10.4135/9781473910751.

Percy-Smith, B., N. P. Thomas, C. O'Kane, and A. Twum-Danso Imoh, eds (2023), *A Handbook of Children and Young People's Participation: Conversations for Transformational Change*, 2nd edn, New York: Routledge.

Spencer, G., ed. (2021), *Ethics and Integrity in Research with Children and Young People*, Leeds: Emerald Publishing.

Westwood, J., C. Larkins, D. Moxon, Y. Perry, and N. Thomas, eds (2014), *Participation, Citizenship and Intergenerational Relations in Children and Young People's Lives: Children and Adults in Conversation*, London: Palgrave.

Archival Research

Agostinho, D. (2019), 'Archival Encounters: Rethinking Access and Care in Digital Colonial Archives,' *Archival Science*, 19: 141–65. https://doi.org/10.1007/s10502-019-09312-0.

Colavizza, G., T. Blanke, C. Jeurgens, and J. Noordegraaf (2021), 'Archives and AI: An Overview of Current Debates and Future Perspectives,' *Journal on Computing and Cultural Heritage*, 15 (1): 1–15. https://doi.org/10.1145/3479010.

Odumosu, T. (2020), 'The Crying Child: On Colonial Archives, Digitization, and Ethics of Care in the Cultural Commons,' *Current Anthropology*, 61 (S22): S289–302. https://www.journals.uchicago.edu/doi/10.1086/710062.

Sharing Stories

Bishop, R. S. (2003), 'Reframing the Debate About Cultural Authenticity', in D. L. Fox and K. G. Short (eds), *Stories Matter: The Complexity of Cultural Authenticity in Children's Literature*, 25–37, Urbana, IL: National Council of Teachers of English.

Booth, W. C. (1988), *The Company We Keep: An Ethics of Fiction*, Berkeley: University of California Press.

Loza, R. (2018), 'Authentic', *Brock Education Journal*, 27 (2): 29–33.

Mo, W., and W. Shen (1997), 'Reexamining the Issue of Authenticity in Picture Books', *Children's Literature in Education*, 28 (2): 85–93.

Yokota, J. (1993), 'Issues in Selecting Multicultural Children's Literature', *Language Arts*, 70 (3): 156–67.

4

Challenges, barriers and possibilities, edited by Courtney Weikle-Mills and Xu Derong

4.1 Introduction by Courtney Weikle-Mills

In preparing this book, editor Kimberley Reynolds requested information from students and early career scholars about their experiences in the field. Their answers revealed that researchers in children's literature studies face many of the same challenges as colleagues in other fields – from defending the significance of our work in a time of dwindling public support for the humanities to navigating a depressed job market to, as Frauke Pawels, a senior researcher at the University of Antwerp, crisply puts it, 'balancing . . . my personal values with the demands of the academic system (and its many neo-liberal, capitalist aspects)'.

Pawels also identifies a challenge specific to the children's literature field and its original formation around an Anglocentric canon, namely how those from other national, linguistic and cultural traditions can position themselves as experts 'in a field that has for long been driven and thrived in a mainly Anglo-oriented world'. For her, this raises the even more important question of how to balance contributions to 'the society that surrounds you in real life' with the 'international publications to be able to maintain an academic position', where there is pressure to use English as a common language and expectation of engaging with English-language scholarly and literary traditions. In addition to this Anglophone bias, the association of childhood with people who are white, middle-class and able-bodied has imposed barriers to researchers working outside of these parameters. This adds to the structural inequalities that such researchers often face within academia in general. The compounding, intersectional challenges of working on underacknowledged and under-resourced areas within a field already referred to (in the first three issues of the flagship journal, *Children's Literature*) as 'the great excluded' can feel daunting indeed.

For decades, scholars have been tenaciously challenging the field's own tendency to exclude by pointing to the existence of multiple traditions and experiences of childhood. Although the idea of multiple childhoods, first proposed in the 1990s, is generally accepted as a framework, as Sarada Balagopalan points out, assumptions about normative childhood continue to generate privilege for some childhoods and scholarly approaches over others. This at times results in empty celebrations of diversity rather than true transformation, a tendency highlighted by the '#WeNeedDiverseScholars' Forum held at a Children's Literature Association Conference and later published in *The Lion and the Unicorn*. The forum called for 'an academic praxis that moves beyond acknowledging the value of diversity . . . to active inclusion, active listening, and active awareness' (79). Aligning with these efforts to expose and alleviate the field's limitations – work we should all be doing – this chapter centres on people who face discrimination or other challenges in their scholarship related to cultural and linguistic backgrounds, race and disability, emphasizing constructive directions, methods and solutions. We begin with a section discussing the marginalization of the children's literature field through a wide lens that takes the international community of scholars into account (Section 4.2.1) before turning to a case study that addresses how to counter marginalization *within* the field (Section 4.2.2). Further sections and case studies attend to challenges related to race (Section 4.3), disability (Section 4.4) and cross-cultural, cross-linguistic study and communication (Section 4.5). Overall, the contributors argue that challenges and barriers can present valuable possibilities meaningfully to transform the field.

4.2 Challenging the marginalization of and within the field

4.2.1 Issues around international marginalization of the field by Xu Derong

When researchers embark on research in children's literature, they often discover that this field tends to be marginalized. In many cultures, there are few, if any, key journals dedicated solely to children's literature research. In China and Romania, for example, there are no existing journals exclusively for academic research on writing for children and young people (CYP), while in Poland and Turkey[1] there are only two important journals devoted to this field. This common situation poses challenges to researchers, though these are offset by the many opportunities for new research outlined in Chapter 2. In the following, I will share two ideas that may help researchers establish themselves in the field of children's literature.

Develop your niche

It has been widely agreed that the most effective way to win respect and recognition in a seemingly dismissive academic culture is to bring impressive depth and profundity to your research – to make it 'eye-opening'. Though areas of research differ, the standards by which solid research is judged are universal.

[1]With thanks to Daniela Hăisan, Michal Borodo and Büşra Yaman for the provision of information in Romania, Poland and Turkey, respectively.

In order to create such depth and profundity in their research, researchers need to develop their own research 'niche' through continuous observation and consistent investigation of a specific research area or topic. For example, translation studies of children's literature is a specific research area that needs years of experience both in terms of translation practice and theoretical thinking. Quite different from translating for an adult audience, translating for children requires translators to understand the particular literary mechanisms that make children's literature children's literature and the special needs of the target child readers. With those issues in mind, researchers need to pinpoint specific topics, such as the reproduction of style in translation, and focus on solutions to these in their own cultural settings. By continuously providing innovative thinking and effective solutions to the central issues of a specific area in children's literature, researchers will gradually establish their reputation as leading figures in areas they have helped to develop. The growing number of established academic figures in children's literature research is steadily improving the status of children's literature research in the academic arena.

Offer something new

To boost the recognition of children's literature research, it is advisable to choose topics that both resolve some fundamental questions about writing for CYP and resonate with the mainstream academic community. Such a combination is not only possible but also feasible, particularly for those with an academic background including areas outside of children's literature studies. Take Professor Zhu Ziqiang as an example. When he was new to the field of children's literature, he chose to study the relationship between Chinese children's literature and China's modernization. He devoted his doctoral dissertation to this topic, and his monograph, *Chinese Children's Literature and China's Modernization* (中國兒童文學與現代化進程), studies the nature, development and trend of Chinese children's literature by putting Chinese children's literature in the context of China's modernization process.

This topic is of interest to both researchers who are interested in Chinese children's literature and those who are interested in China's modernization and the development of modernity. This book, the most quoted monograph in Chinese children's literature research, demonstrates how rewarding it can be to combine the key issues in children's literature research with those in other areas of academia.

Of course, there are many approaches to making such combinations. One possible approach involves the reinterpretation of classic works by renowned literary figures from the perspective of children's literature. Such works include fairy tales by Anatole France, *Platero and I* by Juan Ramón Jiménez and *The Nutcracker* by E. T. A. Hoffmann, to name just a few. Investigation of such works helps to reveal the potential depth and breadth of children's literature writing; it also helps to shed new light on works by often-studied authors. Another possible approach is to look into how highly regarded thinkers see and value children's literature. For example, in China, notable figures such as Liang Qiaochao, Lu Xun, Zhou Zuoren and Mao Dun unanimously highlighted the importance of children's literature, which could help to inspire and educate the younger generation and mould a new generation of world citizens. Their thoughts on the importance of children's literature help people to understand how children's literature was viewed in the critical periods in history and how it could be a source of inspiration for today's world (see Section 1.1). Again, such research not only enhances the profile of children's literature research, but also brings new perspectives to studies of influential thinkers.

4.2.2 Case study: Dismantling barriers through reclaiming intellectual sovereignty by Marilisa Jiménez García

I recently had the privilege of presenting at the annual Modern Language Association (MLA) in a panel called 'Children's Literature under the Long Shadow of Imperialism'. As I walked in, I was delighted to see a group of

Filipino, Indian and Puerto Rican rising scholars, some of whom said that my work inspired their studies. Ten to fifteen years ago, I was a graduate student and teacher struggling to have conversations about the US Empire and its relationship to youth literature. Many wanted to talk about race and racism, but eyes would glaze over when hearing the words 'imperialism' with relationship to the United States. When the field willingly hosts a panel on the US Empire, it is clear that attitudes have shifted.

The struggle over Empire is a struggle for language and space. The biggest trick of the US Empire, and specifically its non-continental expansion, described by José Martí as an 'octopus', has been US geographers, historians and policy makers' inability to admit its existence (Immawar, 2022). Yet, the consequences for millions of Filipinos, Puerto Ricans, Hawaiians and Alaskans are often felt through how imperial and colonial practices rendered their entire communities, their texts, artefacts and literacies invisible. Indeed, articulating and locating the US Empire in youth literature often causes all sort of slippages. For example, I remember speaking to someone who complemented my work on 'nonwestern' literature. Immediately, I said, 'You realise Puerto Rico is in the West. Do you mean the Global South?' Indeed, some of what I do with undergraduate and graduate students in my classes is to consider intellectual and research terms and their limits, and to always know that those terms are rooted in social and historical movements and commitments. Terms help us name and see – they also help us ignore.

Writing about the Global South and non-canonical texts in American, Latin American and English studies meant that I was not hired for traditional academic positions until I was able to create a publishing context for myself. As both a scholar of the Global South and of Ethnic Studies, who works with youth literature, I recommend researchers hoping for a better understanding of racial and social justice through this body of texts to understand that the narrative of US Empire needs to be distrusted in various ways. There are four steps to this process, the first being the recognition and acceptance of the United States as a settler colony rather than a nation of immigrants, and the Latinx population in the United States as a 'harvest of empire' (Gonzalez, 2000). Indeed, the United States is actually a layered settler colony with various conquered regions as remnants of Dutch, French, Spanish and British settlers. Often, the US Empire is seen as a continuation of Britain rather than of various imperial legacies, languages and literacies. The second step relates to the first in terms of distrusting US exceptionalism, which is often tied to notions of the United States as a benevolent conqueror and not an occupier of lands that, in certain cases as with Hawaii, it took illegally. Literature testifying to US land occupation by communities such as Indigenous and Latinx are often hidden behind a veil because of the lack of admission of past and ongoing colonial projects, including climate crisis and disaster responses. The third step comes through understanding that these varied settler colonial projects also cause colliding racial paradigms and construction of race within colonialisms and imperialisms (Vasconsuelo, 1925; Roman and Flores, 2009). For example, increasing numbers of writers of colour, such as Ibi Zoboi and Elizabeth Acevedo, are asking us to look at the AfroLatinx and AfroCaribbean descendants who do not fit into colonial categories created by the traditional US Census. Similarly, the fourth step lies in understanding how competing colonialisms also left a legacy of language injustice often through US education policy, which racialized language itself (Roman and Flores, 2009).

My own position in the academy has undergone various translations as I have gone from full-time researcher in a Puerto Rican Studies research institute, to tenured professor in Latinx and Latin American Studies, to director and founder of an interdisciplinary research institute, to Associate Professor of Children's Literature. It is always interesting to see what assumptions academic and public audiences make about what I know and what I don't know, depending on my academic appointment. My recommendation for bringing down barriers in the field include supporting graduate students and junior faculty who are interested in delving deeper into the work of US Empire. A lens that I particularly recommend is Ethnic Studies because it represents the movement of US colonized people towards intellectual sovereignty. In the

United States, this partners with K-12 (kindergarten to twelfth grade) education and teachers and librarians as intellectual labourers and co-conspirators and keeps us grounded in the intellectual history of our communities.

4.3 Race and anti-racism

4.3.1 Integrating Ethnic Studies into children's literature studies by Erica Kanesaka

It would be a mistake to view race as merely a barrier to the study of children's literature. In fact, critical race and ethnic studies approaches to children's literature research represent some of the fastest growing and most vibrant areas of the field today. These developments reflect the contemporary political urgency of unpacking the complex relationships between race and childhood as two deeply entwined social constructs. The expanding body of research at their intersections, moreover, performs the important work of undoing longstanding absences and injustices in academia and in the broader world. While people of colour have been producing literature for children for centuries, the field of children's literature studies centred in the Global North has historically neglected or marginalized many of these texts while glorifying a predominately white canon of children's literature 'classics'. Scholars who assume critical race and ethnic studies approaches to children's literature studies, a sizeable number of whom are people of colour themselves, have concurrently found their research pigeonholed, diminished, and sometimes even vilified by their academic communities and society at large. Although the field has begun to change in recent times, many of these obstacles remain, presenting significant challenges to researchers invested in this vital line of inquiry.

The barriers that suppress a critical investigation of race in children's literature are perhaps some of the best testaments to its urgency and impact.

As evidence, at the time of this writing, recent years have seen the emergence of right-wing panic in the United States over teaching 'critical race theory' in primary schools alongside demands to ban or censor children's books deemed too inflammatory for addressing racial justice. For children's literature scholars, this present moment calls for our historically and culturally informed perspectives to help illuminate the part that writing for CYP has played in creating and sustaining public imaginings of race and racism. Children's books have long been a primary medium through which children come to learn about racial difference, whether negatively through the depiction of racist stereotypes and colonialist fantasies, or more positively through counternarratives that centre the voices of people of colour to present more honest and affirming representations. Given the politically and emotionally loaded nature of childhood, research on race in children's literature not only holds critical importance, but also requires continually confronting a unique set of barriers specific to the subject's sensitivity.

These barriers can at once be intellectual, interpersonal and institutional. The institutional barriers that inhibit research on race in children's literature include the minoritization of race within children's literature studies and vice versa: the minoritization of children's literature within ethnic studies fields, including Black, Latinx, Asian American and Indigenous studies. In very different ways, both children's literature studies and ethnic studies have had to confront false assumptions that their objects of analysis are inferior and unworthy of serious study, and consequently, that their research lacks scholarly rigour. Ethnic studies, for example, has been unfairly viewed as intellectually compromised by its activist aims, as 'me-search', in which scholars of colour navel-gaze about their own experiences. Children's literature studies has comparably been disregarded as unserious in alignment with the notion that children's books are frivolous or transparent in meaning. Despite these commonalities, these fields of study have not always been in alliance, with children's literature remaining a relatively minor topic within ethnic studies. This double minoritization can also mean that institutional structures, such as dissertation, hiring and tenure-and-promotion committees, discourage or disincentivize scholars in formative stages of their careers from pursuing work at the intersections of race and childhood.

Additionally, as many scholars of colour researching at these intersections have observed, those who are leading the way in diversification efforts regularly encounter resistance from within children's literature studies. Following a panel on this topic at the 2016 Children's Literature Association annual conference, in 2017, Sarah Park Dahlen, Laura M. Jiménez, Marilisa Jiménez García and Michelle H. Martin published a forum in *The Lion and the Unicorn* 41(1) that addressed the interpersonal and institutional obstacles they have faced – from barriers in publishing, teaching, and service to everyday micro- and macroaggressions at conferences and elsewhere in their professional lives. Those interested in learning more about racial inequalities and injustices within children's literature studies would be advised to read their work alongside that of Brigitte Fielder, Angel Daniel Matos, Lara Saguisag, Debbie Reese, Ebony Elizabeth Thomas and others who have spoken and written on this subject. Making children's literature studies more diverse in its literary and theoretical investments and in the demographics of its scholars requires reckoning with the field's past and ongoing exclusions while attending carefully to the wisdom of those who came before. Moreover, the energy that built around the panel and forum contributed to the founding of *Research on Diversity in Youth Literature* (*RDYL*), an open-access journal dedicated to publishing scholarship that centres diversity and difference. *RDYL* now represents an excellent and accessible resource for anyone interested in keeping up to date on the latest research on race in children's literature. The journal's success illustrates how calling attention to injustices and inequalities in the field can result in scholars coming together to create meaningful change.

In part because of the previously mentioned barriers impeding research on race in children's literature, there remain many rich possibilities for future growth in this area. While a significant portion of the extant research on race in children's literature has been advanced by scholars of education, library science, literary and cultural studies, approaches that investigate nuances of language and image within ethnic children's literature have been less developed, along with historical studies of literature produced prior to the contemporary period. Research that moves across children's literature and ethnic studies to think critically about multicultural representation – not just as an important consideration for thinking about who is represented and what children should read, but as an ideological construct that can sometimes promise greater visibility without bringing about meaningful political change. In other words, while movements for more diverse children's books hold undeniable importance, children's literature studies cannot stop at participating in these efforts but must also grapple with the critiques of empty multiculturalism that are integral to many ethnic studies fields. In addition to advocating for more diverse children's books, research on race in children's literature might increasingly contribute to our historical and theoretical understandings of the ties between race and childhood. Such research might, for example, explore questions of intersectionality, imperialism, colonialism, globalization, comparative racializations and environmental issues. There is also the need for further studies that expand our scholarly knowledge of race in children's literature by moving outside the Black-white binary and looking beyond the confines of Great Britain and the United States.

This is not to say that little work has been done on these topics. To claim that ethnic children's literature is only a recent development and exists as a relatively new subfield within children's literature studies would represent a critical erasure, neglecting the depth of this body of work and the hard-won contributions of the scholars who have created space for such research to flourish today. Scholars who are interested in undertaking research on race in children's literature would therefore benefit from taking the time to dig into the archives (see Chapter 5), read broadly across the scholarship, and engage meaningfully with both ethnic studies and the scholars already doing this type of work within children's literature studies. Because the barriers to studying race in writing for CYP will almost certainly persist for some time to come, building and sustaining a community that supports this research – together with the well-being of the scholars who do it – will prove essential to the future of children's literature studies.

4.3.2 Case study: Critical race counterstorytelling as an anti-racist method by Ebony Elizabeth Thomas

How we engage in others' words and experience others' worlds through stories varies according to who we are. As Paulo Freire and Donaldo Macedo note in their influential book *Literacy: Reading the Word and the World* (1987): 'Reading does not consist merely of decoding the written word or language; rather, it is preceded by and intertwined with knowledge of the world' (29). Unfortunately, many books encountered by CYP are not intended for a diverse readership, failing to sufficiently recognize and honour the differences in our young people's words and worlds (Thomas, 2016: 112). At a time when children and adolescents around the globe hail from different backgrounds and lived experiences, the diversity gap in children's literature is closing, but remains a persistent issue. Recent scholarship attests to the ways that reading painful stories can unwittingly perpetuate trauma for young people from marginalized backgrounds (Dumas, 2014). Sometimes, even tales that are culturally authentic can unwittingly index painful moments. The hurt can sometimes be compounded when an author or screenwriter is not from the culture in question. This may render even the best narrative intentions futile.

We read and listen to stories not only to be informed, but also as a way to enter worlds that are not like our own. Stories provide mirrors, windows and doors into other existences, both real and imagined (Bishop, 1990). A sense of the infinite possibilities inherent in fairy tales, fantasy, science fiction, comics and graphic novels draws children, teens and adults from all backgrounds to speculative fiction (also known as the fantastic). Today's youth and young adults are frequently using the networked communities of social media to create new narratives of the imagination (Thomas and Stornaiuolo). However, when people of colour seek passageways into the fantastic, we often discover that the doors are barred. Even the very act of dreaming of worlds-that-never-were can be challenging when the known world does not provide many liberatory spaces.

In *The Dark Fantastic: Race and the Imagination in Youth Literature, Media, and Culture* (2019), I argued that the presence of Black characters in speculative fiction (across genre and mode) creates a dilemma. The way that this dilemma is most often resolved is by enacting symbolic and/or actual violence against the character as the inevitable resolution of the narrative. This is what readers of the fantastic expect, for it mirrors the spectacle of symbolic violence against the endarkened and Othered in our own world. The 'dark fantastic' is my term for the role that racial difference plays at the frontiers of our fantastically storied imaginations. Influenced by fantasy writers from C. S. Lewis to Tracy Deonn, fantasy theorists from Tzvetan Todorov and Brian Attebery to Farah Mendlesohn, and author-critics from Toni Morrison to Kevin Young, I defined the fantastic as inclusive of fantasy fiction, alongside all stories-that-never-were, whether they are classified as fairy tales, horror, superhero comics, 'soft' science fiction, alternate histories or otherwise. Words matter, and the fantastic has multiple resonant connotations. The fantastic evokes the wonder of stepping into a world-that-never-was, and immersing yourself in it in a way that (for me) speculative fiction does not quite capture.

The Dark Fantastic used a critical race counterstorytelling approach to think about fantasy. First theorized by legal scholars Derrick Bell, Kimberle Crenshaw, Mari Matsuda, Richard Delgado and others in the 1980s, critical race theory emerged from the need to explain the persistence of racial discrimination and social suffering in the United States long after the classical Civil Rights movement ended. Critical race theory uses storytelling and personal narrative as method, which is part of a long intellectual tradition in African American letters beginning with the slave narratives. In order to bring critical race theory into conversations about children's and young adult literature and media, the counterstories of readers must be foregrounded.

The Dark Fantastic brings this rich critical tradition to bear through analysis of the fantastic as both genre and social construct, narrating my experiences as a Black woman interactant before moving to the interplay among the voices of texts, critics and researchers, and finishing with the voices of the characters of colour themselves. Instead of focusing my literary analyses on White protagonists, I shed light on these stories from the perspectives of dark girls on the margins. Counterstorying from the points of view of these 'girls on the side', I explored the fantastic through four stories, four fantastic worlds and four Black girl protagonists. In my chapter on *The Vampire Diaries* book series and television show, for example, I examined the way that Bonnie Bennett is positioned vis-à-vis beauty and desirability politics, privileging her story over that of White protagonist Elena Gilbert. As I turned towards analysing racial innocence in a chapter on *The Hunger Games*, it was Katniss' young friend Rue, not Katniss herself, whose positionality I sought to privilege. I show how the marginalization of dark fictional girls within these transmedia texts is analogous to the marginalization of people of colour in schooling and society. Taking a critical race perspective shed light on how race in the imagination can bend such tales at the seams, contorting both space and time.

I strongly believe that children's books and media can change the world. This belief was sparked many years ago when I read Canadian scholar Shaobo Xie's call for a decolonized children's literature: 'Children are perhaps the most victimized and most urgently need to be postcolonized, not so much because they are the most colonized as because they are most violently subjected to colonialist ideas of Otherness at the most formative years of their life' (13). I agree with Xie that although texts for CYP remain undertheorized and undervalued objects of scholarship, critique of books, films, magazines, websites, comics and graphic novels intended for CYP is indeed one of the most effective postcolonial and critical projects in the long run, for 'the world ultimately belongs to children'. As a 23-year-old English language arts teacher in Detroit, I was electrified by his dream that 'if today's children . . . are encouraged to understand and appreciate racial/ethical difference, that would tremendously expedite the progression toward a globalized postcoloniality' (13). Since then, I have consciously constructed a career with this goal in mind, first, as a teacher, then, as a scholar studying the unique roles of adolescent literacy, classroom discourse, and especially youth literature in redefining society and enacting social change.

In the near future, I anticipate the publication of my first novel, combining my love of young adult fantasy with my passion for history, advocacy and social justice. Through emancipated imaginations, endarkened and made whole, I believe that the literary landscape for our young people can indeed be made anew, leaving ample room for new readings of the word and the world.

4.4 Disability and crip engagement with children's literature by Ariel Baker-Gibbs

An inclusive approach to disability in children's literature studies starts with questions about what you perceive as disability and how, when, and if you perceive it. In the first chapter of Louise Fitzhugh's 1964 *Harriet the Spy*, Harriet's nanny, Ole Golly, takes her and her friend Sport to visit her mother, and they realize that 'this lady isn't very bright':

> "Behold, Harriet," Ole Golly said, "a woman who never had any interest in anyone else, nor in any book, nor in any school, nor in any way of life, but has lived her whole life in this room, eating and sleeping and waiting to die" (23).

Why might Fitzhugh have chosen to start a novel about a precocious eleven-year-old writer with her first encounter with an intellectually disabled – and fat – person, and to have this character's own daughter represent her this way? What effect does that have as it serves as the groundwork for the remainder of the novel? And what difference does it make to us that Mrs Golly is never named disabled as such, even though the descriptions of her character make it abundantly clear that she is?

While it can be easy to identify a disabled character (though many disabilities are not visible or obvious), it's questions of ability and disability that underlie everything, because they illustrate the truths and frustrations of having a body, which is one thing no one can avoid. No person can avoid having been a child, either. In this sense, the study of writing for CYP lends itself uniquely to a disability lens. Children are highly aware of how their bodies must navigate the world and the systems of power that contain or threaten them. As crip scholar Ellen Samuels observes, 'Some of us contend with the impairments of old age while still young; some of us are treated like children no matter how old we get'. The question of what it means to be a child and to be treated like one is at the heart of children's literature and its study. Crip and disability studies and children's literature studies are equally bound up with problems of agency, age, bodies and time.

How ability and disability are valued and the metrics by which they are named have fluctuated over the centuries. The only reason there is a discussion of disability as an aspect of the study of writing for the young today is because we have the current formulations that invite scholars, disabled or not, to talk about it – and they serve us for good and for ill. As disabled scholars, the biggest fact of ability and disability in the twenty-first century is that in the world of assimilationist access most easily marked by the 1990 Americans with Disabilities Act, one's body is a site of legal dispute and cost-assessment. Barriers to the study of children's literature for disabled scholars are thus easy to enumerate: buildings, materials, conversations, hovering price tags and other people.

The pathways to showing one's face and mind in academia and the barriers that these pathways naturally form are complex at each stage: diagnosis, documentation, negotiation, self-justification, coordinating the access and making it physically happen. The language around this suggests that it is a bodiless, interaction-less experience. It is not. Each of these stages requires the approval, permission and cooperation of individual people who are more often than not systemically primed to be loath to do it. This perpetual state of contingency takes up time and energy. But this contingency is also the seed of the most important solution to this experience: the power of collective action and communal interdependence. When a community – of colleagues, classmates, advisors, professors, departments, abled, disabled – shares the responsibilities of access, negotiation and advocacy, it is nowhere as easy for the solitary disabled person to disappear again.

The flip side of this is representation. In literature, and that for CYP especially, we are hard pressed to find disability that is not a trope of some kind, that doesn't *represent* something. Everyone loves an overcoming narrative, in which a disabled person manages to do something despite their disability; or better, the supercrip, a disabled person who compensates for their disability with other amazing powers. Other favourites include the disabled villain, the symbolically cathartic figure, the disposable character, the sexless saint, the inspiration porn and so on. Since the ground-breaking work of disability scholars such as Lennard Davis, Rosemarie Garland Thomson, Tobin Siebers or Robert McRuer, or of Sharon L. Snyder and David T. Mitchell in their account of the ways disability functions in literature in *Narrative Prosthesis: Disability and the Dependencies of Discourse* (2000), disability scholarship has developed to call for more systemic reading techniques. In crip-of-colour critique, formulated by Jina B. Kim in 2017, the looming presence of the state, environment and infrastructure is illuminated by disability as it intersects with race, much in the same way that some of my fellow contributors have identified that it is illuminated by childhood. A similarly system-oriented rhetorical development appears in Elizabeth Wheeler's 2019 monograph, *Handiland: the Crippest Place on Earth*, in which Wheeler imagines a perfect world, environment and infrastructure for disabled children through the lens of children's literature in part by redefining apparent inconveniences or weaknesses – such as Harry Potter's headaches – as what they are in truth: disabilities. Children's literature's history of pedagogical function means such representations and acts of reading become particularly fruitful sites for interrogation: how are these bodies written? How else might they be? And how might they be read?

There are many ways that disability takes form, and many ways in which having a body shapes movement through life. Some people are born disabled, others become disabled through illness, events or age. Some are at the whim of unpredictable episodes or flareups, others simply have immutable facts about their body. Some people need a rigid routine, others require constant adaptation. And these experiences of disability are complexly inflected by race, gender, sexuality, body weight and shape, ethnicity, immigration status, culture, language and more. The diagnostic pleasures of terms such as blind, deaf or hard-of-hearing, physical disabilities, autism, ADHD, intellectual disability, developmental disability, cognitive processing disorder, gastrointestinal illness, chronic illness, chronic pain, cancer, depression, anxiety, mental illness, autoimmune disease, long Covid . . . are one thing, the material realities are another. Are, for example, primary materials such as novels, picturebooks, illustrations or audio content captioned or accessible to those with visual impairments or those for whom turning pages is difficult? Can neurodiverse, deaf, hard-of-hearing, or people with other auditory processing or communication disorders participate easily in these academic gatherings? How wide are the doors to research spaces such as archives and collections? How heavy? Can a person in a wheelchair pass through?

Bodily experience and disability shape access to the tools and spaces of academia. Building a community capable of bringing about the changes necessary to make access and inclusion automatic takes time. This is not just about the barriers that disabled people face as a sequestered group, but also about how to recognize and interrogate the ceaseless calculus of ability and disability as they weigh both in the literature we study and in the lives we share. Often in the not always retroactive reading of literature – as I do with *Harriet the Spy* and might do with any children's book – it is tempting to diagnose speculatively, but the more powerful act of reading is to recognize what and how people are doing what they're doing. How hard is it for them to do it? Or how easy? And what aren't they doing? What kind of value is being ascribed to these abilities and to these people right now, both practically and narratively?

4.5 Barriers and opportunities for international researchers

4.5.1 International researchers' contributions to the field by Sreemoyee Dasgupta

The claim that internationalism provides alternative perspectives within a discipline is not a mere platitude when it comes to children's literature. The concept of multiple childhoods across differing national histories and literatures has been permeating the field over the last two decades (see Sarada Balagopalan, Emer O'Sullivan, Zohar Shavit). Given that before the formation of the United Nations, about 80 per cent of the world's nations were European colonies, engaging with childhoods and children's literatures of large swathes of the world necessarily entails accounting for the history of colonial empires and their legacies. As leaders in global higher education, the United States and the United Kingdom attract students from all over the world. They bring with them their unique cultural upbringings and histories, providing 'insider' knowledge that is still missing in children's literature scholarship, especially from the Global South, where the majority of post-colonies are based.

Children's literature scholarship is also dominated by a focus on Anglophone texts and scholarship in English. The domination of the English language is in large part due to the history of British imperialism, as well as the intertwining of globalization with neocolonialism. International students often come from a bilingual or multilingual culture, which is an invaluable tool for accomplishing decolonial and subaltern methodology. Linguistic diversity, combined with the knowledge that comes from being cultural insiders and a comparative methodology can be an extremely effective decolonizing tool. While the target audience for such scholarship is mostly academics, their percolation to librarians, children's book authors, publishers, agents, reviewers, award committees, can combine to increase decolonial diversity within commercial children's book trade as well.

I mention decolonial diversity because the concept of diversity and DEI (diversity, equity and inclusion) varies across national spaces. The nuts and bolts of achieving diverse academic scholarship depend on a country's national demographics and colonial history. However, there must be a balance between regional and global diversities, between the many national understandings of diversity and international and transnational definitions of the term. Within children's literature scholarship, area specialists have done a good job of carving out the scope of diversity within their sphere. International students have the tools to add the global, transnational perspectives to these understandings that are crucial to unearthing the patterns in the circulation and discursive deployment of childhood across the world. Transnational and comparative methodologies can be decolonial in their very conception, while also providing opportunities for North-South and South-South collaboration, enhancing decolonial processes by promoting alternative epistemologies and understandings of childhood that are crucial for the development of a nation's futurity. Global understandings of childhood shape policy documents such as the United Nations Convention on the Rights of the Child (UNCRC), and international students are key to the formulation of these concepts.

4.5.2 Case study: An autoethnography of postcolonial academic ambition by Sreemoyee Dasgupta

This is an attempt to pen down a commonplace story of postcolonial ambition. During my childhood in the 1990s, middle-class Bengal still judged success by the ability to travel 'elsewhere' for education and work. Other Indian metropolitan cities were lucrative, but the pinnacle was the developed Western 'abroad'. While dreams were fine things to have in postcolonial India, success was always deeply embedded in a haloed materiality emanating from the developed West. So naturally, when I chose academia as my profession, I looked to the Anglo-American academic institutions within which my professors were educated. As with other middle-class girls with critical training limited to high-school textbooks, professors at the premier English department in my city represented the prestige and cult status of aspiration.

None of my educational experiences at the 'premier' institute I had attended had prepared me for the realities of graduate school abroad. In my undergraduate programme, we were told that one either knew how to write/analyse or one didn't. There was no instruction on composition and craft; I had rarely received any feedback on my writing beyond identifying proofreading errors. I had a vague idea of what a thesis was; formulating one within an academic piece was beyond my capabilities. I had studied in a lecture-exam system; we read primary texts just before exams and regurgitated lecture notes for our answers. I was unprepared for seminar style graduate coursework, overwhelmed by the weekly readings and assignments, and resorted to recapitulating secondary criticism instead of developing original ideas for my papers. In short, I was clueless. No wonder then that I didn't recognize the impending academic trauma narrative I would have to negotiate to finish my degree. There is no programme which takes the time to explain the differences in pedagogic style and supervision to international graduate students. Doctoral work in India and the United Kingdom proceeds very differently from doctoral work in the United States, with far less coursework and more individual research. Each system has its pros and cons, but across the board, there is no guidance on how to adapt to the system in which students find themselves. It was only retrospectively that I realized my mistakes. I did eventually find my way, but it took time.

Papers galore in psychology and social science journals proclaim the vulnerability of international students to loneliness and isolation. The situation is particularly acute for those from non-Anglophone countries, having to not only negotiate an unfamiliar geo-cultural terrain away from their loved ones, but also embody racial difference in the very shape of the words they speak. Global Englishes and their accents might be pervasive in scholarship, but in reality, it will take the intervention of educational institutions and student organizations, understanding teachers and advisors, as well as conscientious and open-minded peers to alleviate the pressures of academic ambition. Publications such as this one pave the way for the starting point: the need for acknowledging the trials of international students, and for mentors, teachers, academic departments and university immigration offices to recognize the connection between the academic and the emotional work international students have no choice but to balance.

The need for conversations that spell out exactly what international students need to know, both within their departments and fields and within 'Western academia' is long overdue, which is why I write here what I wish I had known above all else: higher education has a 'hidden curriculum', rules which are never written and expectations that are never explicitly stated. A higher education degree is as much about understanding and applying this hidden curriculum as it is about the contents of your research. Only by doing so is it possible to avoid some of the pitfalls international students face in their programmes. Doing a PhD abroad is also a hustle; international students are often barred from many funding opportunities, and many workspaces are reluctant to sponsor a work visa. Being constantly on the lookout for opportunities and funding can be tiring, but it can also provide transferable professional skills. The trick is to think and look globally, while knowing your strengths on a global market. My biggest takeaway: in the absence of other mitigating factors, it is only resilience and initiative that will take you a long way, sometimes even all the way.

4.5.3 Selecting a research topic as an international student by Anna Katrina Gutierrez

For international students aiming to contribute to and make their mark in children's literature scholarship, selecting a research topic can be as pivotal as the turning point in a classic fairy tale. The right choice – finding your 'niche' as described in Section 4.2.1 – can open doors to academic recognition and career opportunities, while aligning one's research with personal passions can fuel perseverance and satisfaction.

Self-assessment and goal setting

Embarking on an academic journey begins with introspection. It's crucial to reflect on why children's literature captivates you. Is it the art of storytelling? The psychological impact on young minds? Or, perhaps, it's the cultural narratives that these stories transport across borders? As an international student, you may want to consider your country's children's literature: what makes it unique or fascinating, and the role it plays in local and global contexts. Next, evaluate your academic strengths. Are you inclined towards literary analysis, cultural studies or educational psychology (see Section 2.1)? Your strengths will guide your research methodology. Finally, consider your goals. Do you aspire to reform educational curricula or contribute to literary criticism? For an international researcher, it is always worth aiming to develop research that engages and enriches international perspectives while uplifting and empowering your local research community. Aligning your interests, strengths and goals will illuminate the path to a research topic that is meaningful.

Overcoming challenges as an international student

As discussed in Chapters 1 and 2, children's literature is a dynamic field with diverse sub-genres and interdisciplinary connections. As an international student, you bring a unique perspective to the table. Immerse yourself in the host country's literary culture while staying connected to your roots. This dual perspective can reveal gaps in cross-cultural representations or bilingual literature, offering fertile ground for research (see Section 4.5.4). Scholarship in the field often entails looking beyond children's literature and drawing from critical perspectives of related fields of interest, such as cognition studies, globalization studies or queer studies, to name just a few. International students face unique challenges, such as language barriers and cultural differences. Embrace these as opportunities to offer a fresh perspective on children's literature. Your multicultural background can enrich your research, offering insights that might be overlooked by others. Access resources and funding opportunities through your institution, and don't hesitate to seek support from advisors, translators and peer networks. That's what they are there for.

Your internationally inflected niche in children's literature can be a powerful catalyst for academic and career advancement. Explore research collaborations with scholars in your field or partner with children's book authors and illustrators. Internships at publishing houses or educational institutions can provide practical experience and industry connections. Your unique perspective as an international student studying children's literature is an asset. Utilize it to contribute to global conversations in the field.

4.5.4 Addressing language barriers when communicating research by Yu Chengcheng

If you are a researcher delving into children's literature in a non-native language, the selection of a study topic may not just be an academic decision but a reflection of your cultural heritage and intellectual trajectory. The following recommendations aim to help you traverse the broad scope of children's literature scholarship and develop a unique voice in the international academic exchange.

Navigating the terrain of cross-cultural perspectives

For startup researchers seeking to share their work with English-speaking audiences, selecting research topics that illustrate the benefits of harnessing cultural and linguistic strengths can be a strategic choice. As a Chinese scholar, I have published several papers on Chinese children's literature, which has allowed me to engage in the global academic conversation surrounding children's literature. My journey began with an article project that focused on the anthropomorphic approach in Chinese wild animal stories that were translated into English. This initial endeavour paved the way for further investigations, including two articles on 'Eco-translation' to examine the disparities and convergences in ecological sensibilities across languages and cultures. Furthering the cross-cultural academic discourse, I ventured into a comparative analysis that involved juxtaposing the storytelling techniques and degrees of anthropomorphism employed by Chinese and Western authors in the genre of wild animal stories. Each of these research avenues, rooted in a cross-cultural perspective, serves as a gateway to new perspectives and reveals the generic complexities inherent to storytelling and the interplay between languages, cultures and narratives.

Leveraging secondary resources

Ensuring the originality and depth of ideas requires exploration of both domestic and international resources when conducting research. Resources specific to Chinese scholarship, such as Chinese Social Sciences Citation, CNKI (China National Knowledge Infrastructure) and Chinese Doctor Dissertations Full-text Database, can provide valuable localized information. Chapter 2 contains advice on identifying additional resources and databases specific to your research area. While local, country-specific resources such as those in China are important, it is worth underscoring the value of international resources such as JSTOR, Project MUSE and Google Scholar, as well as Google Books, e-book collections from academic publishers and platforms like ProQuest Ebook Central. The use of domestic and international resources can enhance the quality of a literature review and facilitate the identification of research gaps, comparative analysis and the integration of different theoretical frameworks.

Case study: Overcoming language barriers

Ingenuity is indeed required to bridge linguistic gaps and harness global perspectives embedded in your research to resonate with, and be recognized by, the English-speaking academic community and beyond. In my study of Naoko Awa's fairy tales, I conducted a close reading of their English translations to examine the interplay between her works and the European fairy tale tradition. With Japanese beyond my linguistic reach, my research relied heavily on English-language resources, including a dozen English book reviews, and notably, works that discuss Kenji Miyazawa's perspectives on human-animal relationships – a theme echoed in Awa's stories. To better avail myself of my native language resources, my research also drew upon Chinese scholarship on Awa, particularly an MA thesis sourced from the Digital Library of Theses and Dissertations in Taiwan. The thesis presents Chinese translations of Awa's reflections and commentaries on fairy tales, originally in Japanese, that illuminate her environmental sensibilities. By synthesizing textual analysis, biographical context and intercultural perspectives, my interpretation was further informed by Marco Caracciolo's concept of 'slow narratives', the lens of which allowed for a nuanced understanding that bridged narrative form with ecological thematics. This research journey embraced cultural nuances and variations of fairy tales in ways that not only deepened my understanding of Awa's works within the broader tapestry of literature but also demonstrated the rich potential of cross-linguistic study to reveal new dimensions in literary analysis.

4.5.5 Research across cultures: Contrasts in Chinese and Anglophone academic traditions by Shuqin Jiang

Academic conventions vary across different cultures, influencing the way scholars approach research, share knowledge and write papers. The examples here compare Anglophone and Chinese styles of thinking and writing, but the same pertains across cultures to varying degrees.

The most discernible contrast between Anglophone and Chinese academic writing is the differing modes of thought. English-language based thinking tends to be linear, adhering to a direct and sequential approach in organizing and articulating ideas. Writing in English typically follows a top-down pattern, presenting a topic sentence first, followed by supporting details and a restatement of the argument. In contrast, Chinese writing often follows a bottom-up pattern, providing background information first and culminating in the major argument at the end of the paper. Syntactically, Chinese is a paratactic language that emphasizes implicit coherence of meaning over explicit grammatical elements, while English is a hypotactic language that heavily relies on grammatical elements to indicate structural relationships. In Chinese, clauses are placed successively without connectives to specify their logical relationship. Some English readers may find Chinese academic papers perplexing due to the absence of topic sentences, the indirect approach to argumentation and logically loose sentences. After understanding these differences, writers can consider these contrasting modes of thought and structure their writing in accordance with the English pattern when seeking to publish in English.

While the choice of topic has much to do with individual interests, leading international journals will only publish work that is original and fills gaps in our current understanding. So, choose the topic of your research carefully to ensure your work is novel, relevant and interesting. In China, research on children's literature tends to focus on fundamental and general issues, such as its historical context, disciplinary status, research principles and methodologies, likely due to its relatively recent emergence and China's collectivist culture. Conversely, English-language journals, many of which have been in existence for decades and have covered these topics at an earlier stage, have a keen interest in specific topics related to cultural diversity, gender equality, racial and ethnic representation in recent years. While experienced Anglophone scholars also engage in exploring comprehensive topics that provide insightful guidance, commencing with a particular case study can be an advantageous option to newcomers to the field. Note that the case studies should be distinctive while also prompting broader reflection. Delving into extensive theoretical explorations can significantly enhance their scholarly value.

Once you have settled on your subject and commenced the writing process, bear in mind the importance of maintaining an approach that is appropriate for your intended audience. Children's literature studies, as an interdisciplinary field, draws from various disciplines such as literature, education, psychology, history and cultural studies. While some papers may use the IMRaD (Introduction, Methods, Results and Discussion) structure commonly used in STEM (science, technology, engineering and maths) and social sciences, most papers in humanities follow the format of introduction, body and conclusion (for more discussion of writing skills and literature reviews, see Chapter 2).

In China, literature reviews usually provide comprehensive backgrounds and often include historical perspectives. Chinese scholars commonly highlight the contributions of previous researchers while incorporating a holistic view of the subject matter. In contrast, English-language literature reviews focus on recent developments, critical debates and gaps in knowledge, thereby encouraging scholars to adopt a more critical and analytical approach to raise research questions and thesis statements.

If you are targeting English-language journals for a publication, it is essential to ensure that your thesis statement is explicitly stated in the introduction, rather than the conclusion. Moreover, it is crucial that your thesis statement directly addresses the central question or issue you intend to explore. The body of the text should then build the thesis with lucid reasoning and analysis (Section 2.4 discusses writing up research). While the specific structure will depend on your topic and research, a general guideline is to include two or three sections, each focused on a different aspect of the thesis statement. These ideas should unfold in a coherent sequence and be thoroughly substantiated with evidence.

The body of the text contains most of the citations and analysis. Writers use close reading of texts, critical analysis and citations from scholarly sources to back up their claims. In Chinese academic writing about literature, there is a tendency to incorporate flowery language, metaphorical expressions and elaborate descriptions. This may lead to a less direct and concise style, a risk of ambiguity and potential distractions from the main arguments. When writing papers in English, try to use straightforward and precise language to prioritize the clear and logical presentation of ideas. It is helpful to use transitional phrases and cohesive devices to establish logical connections and smooth transitions between sentences and paragraphs. Finally, it is important to summarize the main points of your paper, restate your thesis or research questions and offer a final thought or reflection with a conclusion. Instead of simply repeating what has already been said, strive to offer a broader perspective or suggest the implications of your findings.

Ultimately, an academic essay should not be seen as a rigid framework but as a dynamic tool that adapts to the specific research topic within children's literature and the scholarly journal or platform in which it is published. With global communications, China and the world are learning from each other, leading to fewer differences in academic traditions. Moreover, interdisciplinary research is fostering new modes of enquiry, bridging the gap between various academic writing practices. By embracing these insights, aspiring scholars can navigate the complexities of English academic writing with greater confidence and effectiveness.

4.6 Conclusion by Xu Derong and Courtney Weikle-Mills

As the contributors to this chapter have shown, while barriers to researchers in children's literature are real and numerous, addressing these barriers yields many rich potentials for intellectual inquiry and research sharing. We all stand to benefit as the field becomes more diverse and inclusive.

As it is of paramount importance to make breakthroughs in academic research in any given field, addressing these barriers in the researchers' distinct contexts will help to bring something new to the existing scholarship with 'added academic value'. In light of this common mission for researchers of children's literature in the world, it is suggested to adopt interdisciplinary approaches to tackle research questions that could not be well addressed from a single discipline, including but not limited to issues about children's literature in education and children's cognitive development. Besides, it is also possible to take a transnational perspective to investigate children's literature to see how children's literature has been crossing national and cultural borders for its reception and how people of different cultural backgrounds could communicate with each other because of their common reading of children's works based on the conception that children's literature is not written for a single country; it is created for the well-being of all the human beings.

That said, the barriers we mentioned above constitute not deterrence for children's literature research but potential encouragement. Addressing these barriers not only opens up more possibilities for research, but also brings more prospects for future careers, since promising careers in fields such as library science, publishing, elementary and secondary teaching, and non-profit work all involve children's literature research in interdisciplinary approaches. Addressing our common challenges to improve research in children's literature in the world is a hopeful business, as children's literature is a literature of hope itself.

4.7 FURTHER RESOURCES

Abebe, T. et al. (2023), 'Teaching "Global Childhoods" in Childhood Studies', *Childhood*, 30 (4): 360–79.

Balagopalan, S. (2017), 'Colonial Modernity and the Child Figure', in T. S. Saraswathi, Shailaja Menon and Ankur Madan (eds), *Childhoods in India: Traditions, Trends and Transformations*, 23–43, London: Taylor and Francis.

Bayyurt, Y. and D. Altinmakas (2024), 'Insights into Academic Writing in English as Lingua Franca Contexts', *Research Papers in Language Teaching and Learning*, 14 (1): 81–96.

Bowe, H. and K. Martin (2012), *Communication Across Cultures*, Cambridge: Cambridge University Press.

Caracciolo, M. (2022), *Slow Narrative and Nonhuman Materialities*, Lincoln: University of Nebraska Press.

Cronin, M. (2017), *Eco-translation: Translation and Ecology in the Age of the Anthropocene*, Abingdon: Routledge.

'Diversity Children's Literature Collection' at the Baldwin Library of Historical Children's Literature, University of Florida. https://original-ufdc.uflib.ufl.edu/childlitdiversity.

Eddy, R. and A. Espinosa-Aguilar (2019), *Writing Across Cultures*, Logan: Utah State University Press.

Hanson, K. et al. (2018), '"Global/Local" Research on Children and Childhood in a "Global Society"', *Childhood*, 25 (3): 272–96.

Hu, M. (2014), 'Toward the Understanding of Chinese ESL Writing: An Analysis of the Differences Between Chinese and English Writing Helps to Understand Chinese ESL Writing', *English Today*, 30 (1): 55–9.

International Research in Children's Literature (2008–present).

Jiménez García, M. (2021), *Side by Side: US Empire, Puerto Rico, and the Roots of American Youth Literature and Culture*, Jackson: University Press of Mississippi.

Kinzie, S. (2024), 'Language Ideologies and English for Academic Purposes Writing: A Case in Ontario', *The Canadian Modern Language Review*, 80 (1): 1–21.

Mazak, C. (2019), *Making Time to Write: How to Resist the Patriarchy and Take Control of Your Academic Career Through Writing*, New York: Morgan James Publishing.

McGillis, R., ed. (2000), *Voices of the Other: Children's Literature and the Postcolonial Context*, New York: Garland Publishing.

O'Sullivan, E. (2019), 'Translating Children's Literature: What, for Whom, How, and Why. A Basic Map of Actors, Factors and Contexts', *Belas Infiéis*, 8 (3): 13–35.

Research on Diversity in Youth Literature (2016-present). https://iopn.library.illinois.edu/journals/rdyl/index.

Special Issue on Disabilities and Children's Literature (2013). *Children's Literature Association Quarterly*, 38 (3). https://muse.jhu.edu/issue/28095.

Sharifian, F. ed. (2015), *Handbook of Language and Culture*, London and New York: Routledge.

Slater, K., S. P. Dahlen, M. H. Martin, L. M. Jiménez, and M. J. García (2017), '#WeNeedDiverseScholars: A Forum', *The Lion and the Unicorn*, 41 (1): 93–103.

Snyder, S. L. and D. T. Mitchell (2000), *Narrative Prosthesis: Disability and the Dependencies of Discourse*, Ann Arbor: University of Michigan Press.

Stephens, J. ed. (2017), *The Routledge Companion to International Children's Literature*, Abingdon: Routledge.

Thornber, K. (2012), *Ecoambiguity: Environmental Crises and East Asian Literatures*, Ann Arbor: University of Michigan Press.

Thomas, E. E. (2019), *The Dark Fantastic: Race and the Imagination from Harry Potter to the Hunger Games*, New York: New York University Press.

Wheeler, E. (2019), *Handiland: The Crippest Place on Earth*, Ann Arbor: University of Michigan Press.

You, C. (2022), 'Debatable Genre: Comparative Poetics in the Wild Animal Stories of Ernest Thompson Seton and Shixi Shen', *Neohelicon*, 49 (1): 321–36.

You, C. (2024), 'Who Speaks for Nature? Genre, Gender, and the Eco-translation of Chinese Wild Animals', *Children's Literature in Education*, 55 (2): 179–97. https://doi.org/10.1007/s10583-023-09543-6.

5

Using archives, specialist collections and digital humanities resources by Shih-Wen Sue Chen and Kimberley Reynolds

5.1 Introduction by Sue Chen

Although many major research libraries and institutions are digitizing primary sources (see Table 5.2 and Table 5.3 at the end of this chapter), there are still vast amounts of material that are only available offline, and some may not have been catalogued at all. Thus, archival research can be rewarding as well as challenging. This chapter provides strategies for accessing archives and specialist collections, including the process of locating resources, tips for handling rare or fragile books, manuscripts, correspondence, ephemera and visual material. It includes practical information on how to plan for a research trip and guidelines for gathering, storing, managing and interrogating the materials you collect. Through several case studies, researchers share their experiences working in international archives to uncover and analyse lost materials, trace histories of authors, illustrators, publishers and readers. The chapter also introduces digital humanities methods and provides approaches to designing research projects using big data.

5.2 Locating resources: Digital and physical collections by Lenise Prater

The number and scope of digital and physical collections can be quite overwhelming, making it difficult to find relevant primary or secondary sources for your project. The process of finding and navigating the right databases, libraries or archives often differs depending on what you are researching and in which country. WorldCat is a union catalogue that is a good starting point for finding out which institutions hold copies of materials you are interested in consulting. One tool to locate archival collections is ArchiveGrid, a discovery system focused on archival materials worldwide. Search for people, places and events of interest, and the system will retrieve archival institutions where related primary materials are housed. If you do not speak the language of the country where the archive is located, contacting one of the librarians or archivists may prove to be useful, as currently English is widely used as the lingua franca of research institutions. Sometimes the material you are looking for might be part of non-children's literature collections. You might find it helpful to seek help from listservs such as the International Research Society for Children's Literature (IRSCL) mailing list. As technologies, your research focus and institutional affiliations change, you may need to develop new search strategies.

5.2.1 Collections

Broadly, institutions and databases often curate focused collections that can help streamline your research. There are a range of reasons why a library or archive might hold a particular collection; often institutions can have surprisingly extensive materials that share a theme, form or publication date. University libraries often develop their collections based on the research interests, recommendations and requests of the academics who work there. Another reason why a library might build a collection/archive is that a private collector has donated a substantial existing collection. For example, Monash University Library has the Lindsay Shaw Collection of Australian children's fiction, which the secretary of the Monash Faculty of Education began in 1979 and contributed to until his death. Shin Torigoe, a professor at Waseda University in Tokyo, donated a substantial collection of children's literature to the Governor of Osaka prefecture, leading to the establishment of the International Institute for Children's Literature (IICLO), and Ruth Baldwin's personal collection eventually became the Baldwin Library of Historical Children's Literature at the University of Florida.

Websites for libraries and archives carry information about their collections and give an insight into their specialization(s). If you have identified an important scholar in your area of research, check the library website of the university where that academic works to see if they have a relevant collection. You can also find collections using a general search engine to look up *children's literature* (or your specific research interest) and the name of a relevant university or institution (e.g. *children's literature, Brown University*). Once you have identified a library or archive with a collection relevant to your research, you can search the online catalogues and perhaps plan a research trip (see Section 5.3) in case not all their sources have been (or can be) digitized. It is very difficult to capture, say, a pop-up-book or paper doll book in a digital format.

5.2.2 Databases and digitized resources

Online databases are increasingly important for finding and accessing primary and secondary material. Some databases are open access, and state and/or national libraries from many countries are often involved in developing and maintaining databases that grant access to their nation's children's texts. Many databases, such as CLCD (Children's Literature Comprehensive Database) or the Nineteenth Century UK Periodicals Database, are behind a paywall. University libraries subscribe to a range of these, which you can usually find through the online library guides of any institution with which you are affiliated (these are sometimes called 'Library Guides' 'Subject Guides', 'Libguides', 'Research Guides') or by contacting one of the librarians listed on the website. The International Children's Digital Library, the Baldwin Library of Children's Literature Digital Collection, and the Digitalisierte historische Kinderbücher make digitized children's texts freely available.

5.2.3 How to search

The increasing sophistication of algorithms means that well-crafted keyword searches can yield valuable results. However, algorithms are not neutral and can introduce bias into your research; they tend to prioritize the most clicked sources, not necessarily the most relevant ones. Nevertheless, keyword search strategies are useful, as many databases will not return satisfactory results if, for example, you enter a question into the search bar. Keyword searching is an iterative process. Brainstorming a list of keywords is a good way to begin, but once you find relevant results, take note of how those sources are tagged or labelled in the database and add these terms to your list.

Databases and online library catalogues can have very different search interfaces, so some general tips may not apply to the specific database or catalogue you are using. Many databases will offer an advanced search function with filters and exclusions in drop-down menus or check boxes, which will allow you to search only books, only peer-reviewed articles or only texts from a certain collection. Note: it is important to double-check the results as they are only as good as the metadata in the system, and with databases drawing from so many different places, inconsistencies are common.

Most databases have a dedicated web page with tips on searching their interface and contact information for staff to answer queries. These resources are often invaluable and can refine and streamline your research process.

Below is a short list of institutions with extensive children's literature collections, many of which have online catalogues:

- Cotsen Children's Library, Princeton University (New Jersey)
- De Grummond Children's Literature Collection (Mississippi)
- International Institute for Children's Books (Osaka)
- International Youth Library (Munich)
- Library of Congress Children's Literature Center (Washington DC)
- National Centre for Australian Children's Literature (Canberra)
- Osborne Collection of Early Childhood Books (Toronto)
- Seven Stories, the National Centre for Children's Books (Newcastle upon Tyne)
- The Swedish Institute for Children's Books (Stockholm)
- University of Worcester Library (affiliated with the International Forum for Research in Children's Literature, Worcester).

5.3 Planning research trips by Kimberley Reynolds

Research trips may be necessary at different stages in a project. Whether you are investigating what kind of material is available or delving deeply into a topic, preparation is vital. The list below should help you get the most out of any visit. Broadly the same questions pertain whether you are visiting a local archive/collection or travelling to another city or country.

Once you have identified the items you need to see (see Section 5.2) and the institution that holds them, check the following questions against that institution's website or other published information. Do this well in advance of any trip.

5.3.1 Access

- Is there public access to the collection? If so, on what terms? Is a letter of introduction required? Must you present a particular form of ID or proof of address on arrival? Should you register or make an appointment in advance? Do you need to bring a photograph of yourself? Are there any charges related to your visit?
- What are the opening hours, including days of the week, public holidays and any special closures (e.g. for renovations or training)? Such information is not always provided on websites, so check directly with the institution.
- Where are your materials held and are they all on one site? Many institutions operate across several sites which may be considerable distances from each other.
- Can you reserve materials in advance? How many items can be requested at a time, and how long is the retrieval time for subsequent orders? How many items can you order each day? These factors may affect the length of your visit.
- What support is provided for wheelchair users or those with other mobility aids or requirements?
- What provision is made to support special needs such as visual or hearing impairments? Can you bring your own adaptive technology devices?
- Are there facilities for copying documents? Can you use your own phone/camera/tablet to photograph materials? Is the number of images you can take restricted? Are there restrictions on the use of photos of the archive's materials?

After assembling answers to these questions, you need *immediately* to explore the practicalities of travelling to undertake your research.

5.3.2 Logistics

The institution's location and the number and kind of items you require will determine how long your research trip needs to be. Key questions:

- How far are you travelling and what kind(s) of transport will you use? How much will travel cost, including parking, taxis and similar? Is there parking nearby?
- If travelling internationally, will any visa(s) be required?
- If needed, how much will accommodation and subsistence cost?
- Are there any other relevant archives/collections in the same vicinity?
- What are the total costs of the trip? Does your institution or the destination institution offer any bursaries or fellowships? Are there other funding bodies you can approach? (see Chapter 7)

5.3.3 What to bring

Archives/collections are often cool, so bring something warm. If allowed, you may want to bring: a laptop; camera/phone/tablet; paper and pencils (see Section 5.5.1).

5.4 Approaches to archival research

5.4.1 Big data versus close reading by Paavo Van der Eecken and Lindsey Geybels

Literary scholarship commonly involves human researchers reading and analysing selected materials. However, the expansive nature of literature imposes inherent limitations on what can be covered. These limits manifest in both scope – how much we can read – and focus – what we can keep track of when we read. Given the impossibility of reading every book in existence, it is important to question the representativeness of findings based on a small set of works. Limitations in terms of scope have led scholars to prioritize specific works, often favouring canonical books over others. Franco Moretti (2013) refers to the remaining works as the 'great unread', an immense corpus of underexplored literature.

Literary scholars are traditionally trained to engage in closely reading source materials to uncover deeper meanings behind certain elements in the text. Some important information, however, may not be found deep within a text but at a surface level. Such information or data might appear inconsequential in isolation but becomes significant through repetition. As an illustration: stylometry, the computational examination of writing style, gained significant attention in July 2013. Patrick Juola (2023) foregrounded it by analysing four groups of features, including the distribution of word length and the 100 most common words, in a few English novels, and identifying J. K. Rowling as the true author of the detective novel released under the pseudonym Robert Galbraith.

One way to broaden research in terms of both scope and focus is to employ computational techniques. Computers excel at rapid counting and tracking, making them ideal for uncovering patterns in data. Their use in literary research allows researchers to read texts at a remove, an approach often called distant reading. In children's literature, illustrations and other visual elements also play a vital role in the construction of meaning. Therefore, the approach of distant viewing, currently being propelled by advancements in computer vision – an area of computer science dedicated to enabling computers to identify objects in images and videos – holds great potential for this field.

Scholars such as Taylor Arnold and Lauren Tilton (2023) have shown the benefit of clustering visual materials to create new ways of looking at archival materials. This approach holds great potential for archives of illustrated children's literature as well, allowing scholars automatically to group illustrations based on similar visual features. Their Distant Viewing

Toolkit would be an excellent starting point for researchers interested in the computational study of visual culture since it provides ready-made software to study dominant colours, object detection and other features of interest.

Distant reading and viewing offer alternative perspectives on children's literature, but caution is needed in their application. Computational tools are often mistakenly seen as inherently objective. Methods and models, however, do not exist in a void; they require decision-making from researchers, influencing results. These decisions permeate every stage of a digital pipeline. Why do we use tool A as opposed to tool B? Which parameters do we set, and how do we adapt them during our research? Was any data involved in the creation of the tools we use, and how did this influence the way they work? How do we decide which data to use ourselves, and is the material representative? While computational tools offer advantages, they do not magically enhance objectivity compared to close reading.

As the potential of digital tools, and artificial intelligence specifically, is increasingly recognized in society, it is crucial to avoid getting carried away by the hype. The selection of tools should always be in the service of research questions, and not the other way around. The goal is never complexity for complexity's sake. When implementing computational methods, scholars are obliged to ensure that there is a sound connection between the tool, the data and relevant humanities theories. Failure to do so undermines the legitimacy of findings. This is a significant risk in using computational methods; while results may appear convincing, their value depends entirely on the decisions users make along the way.

Distant viewing and reading are commonly juxtaposed with close viewing and reading. While it is beneficial to consider the differences both in their implementation and affordances, we should be careful not to reduce this comparison to a question of superiority. These are alternative approaches, serving as mutually enriching lenses. Distant analyses, through pattern recognition in data, can both support hypotheses derived from closer examinations and act as guides, pinpointing gaps in our knowledge that require further in-depth analysis.

We have set out the stages in designing and conducting a big data study in Table 5.1.

Table 5.1 Designing a Big Data Study

Although every study possesses distinctive objectives and prerequisites, the key stages outlined below provide a standard example study design.
1. Defining objectives and research questions At the outset, clearly articulate the goals of your big data study by identifying research questions and objectives. This stage involves a comprehensive understanding of the problem at hand and the desired outcomes.
2. Data collection Once objectives are established, embark on collecting relevant data. Big data studies often involve diverse datasets, which may include both structured and unstructured data. Ensuring data quality and ethical considerations are crucial during this stage.
3. Data preprocessing Raw data is rarely pristine and needs to be cleaned and pre-processed to ensure uniformity and compatibility. Clean and normalize texts and transform data into a suitable format for analysis.
4. Model development and analysis Use the appropriate tools and techniques to build models that address your research questions. An exploratory analysis might help you gain insights into the dataset's characteristics. Statistical methods, machine learning algorithms or natural language processing tools may be applied to uncover patterns, trends or correlations within the literary data.
5. Interpretation and conclusion The final stage involves interpreting the results obtained through data analysis and drawing conclusions relevant to the initial problem. Visualizations can be used to clearly communicate the results.

Source: Shih-Wen Sue Chen.

5.4.2 Big data case study: Age construction in fiction by Lindsey Geybels

In my doctoral research on age construction in fiction,[1] I explored the nuanced process of constructing fictional age on two levels. First, through

[1]This research was part of the research project 'Constructing Age for Young Readers', supported by the European Research Council (ERC) under the European Union's Horizon 2020 research and innovation programme.

dialogue and character descriptions, and second, by examining how textual features convey insights into the age of the intended reader. To unravel the relationship between text complexity and age, I analysed a corpus of 700-plus texts for readers of varying ages, from young children to adults. The focus was on basic textual features including average, minimum and maximum word and sentence length. My research encompassed investigations of basic textual features alongside intricate natural language processing, employing self-developed Python programmes. Notably, analyses of surface features such as those in the first part of this case study can also be accomplished with readily available tools such as the online Voyant Tools.

Analysis of textual features revealed a general increase in complexity as the intended reader's age advances, aligning with expectations that literature for older children and adolescents tends to incorporate more complex linguistic structures. However, outliers challenging these norms prompted a return to the text, as seen in the works of Dutch author Joke van Leeuwen. One of her books for nine-year-olds (*Slopie*, 2004) defies age-related expectations by incorporating exceptionally long words, e.g. *honderdvijfennegentigeneenhalfpoten* – a whimsical term for a millipede with a specific leg count. Digital tools efficiently identify and contextualize such linguistic peculiarities.

Moving beyond textual features, I explored the construction of fictional age through character speech by annotating texts, with labelled direct speech linked to character age. Such annotations introduce additional subjectivity, influencing results and showcasing the researcher's role in the distant reading method. Determining fictional characters' ages relies on contextual clues, potentially introducing errors and underscoring the interplay between close and distant reading. For instance, in a study of thirteen young adult novels by British author David Almond, analysis of character speech revealed, among other things, a thematic conflict between distant reading. For instance, in a study of thirteen young adult novels by British author David Almond, analysis of character speech revealed, among other things, a thematic conflict between death and love, with characters of different ages talking more about one of these topics than the other. Words such as 'knife', 'murder', 'killed', 'dead', 'war' and 'hate' distinctly characterize adolescent speech, while 'peace' and 'love' are more prevalent in the speech of older/adult characters.

This case study exemplifies the dynamic interplay between the efficiency of the analysis of big data and the diligence of close reading in children's literature studies. The following case study offers an alternative approach to using digital tools to interrogate large bodies of textual material.

5.4.3 Case study: Digital Humanities and children's literature research by Haifeng Hui

Digital Humanities (DH) is not inherently tied to children's literature research, nor is its incorporation an attempt to follow academic trends. Instead, the intersection of these fields stems from two primary motivations: first, the evolution of DH itself, which seeks to refine and justify its applications across various branches of the humanities, and second, children's literature's ongoing quest for new theoretical frameworks and research methodologies.

What Digital Humanities offers children's literature

So, what unique edge or lens does Digital Humanities bring to children's literature studies? At its current stage, the strength of digital humanities lies in its application to distant reading, which involves the exploration, identification, and mining of textual patterns and stylistic features that often escape the naked eye and the short-term memory of literary critics. This method is particularly useful for uncovering patterns in narration, rather than content. For example, the word 'hand' might play a crucial role in a children's novel, both thematically and at the local level of the text. However, recalling and identifying every instance of this word's occurrence would be an arduous and time-consuming task. Even when a critic manually copies every instance, a DH tool can easily surpass this human effort by providing a comprehensive list of all usages, including details such as collocations, syntactical structure, distribution patterns and so on. But what should we do if we want to examine the usage in ten, a hundred or thousands of novels? More complex DH tools, particularly those that involve Python and Natural Language Processing (NLP), can analyse huge amounts of data.

Currently, the most suitable NLP and DH tools for children's literature research include topic modelling, sentiment analysis, computational stylistic analysis and social network analysis. Each of these tools brings a new dimension to the analysis of children's literature, which would be difficult or impossible to achieve through traditional methods.

Topic modelling

Topic modelling can identify themes across literary periods spanning hundreds of years and involving tens of thousands of works. This is a task beyond the capacity of human readers, as it requires processing large-scale datasets. Topic modelling can not only reveal topics across different works and time periods but also trace how these topics evolve over time. It gives scholars a broad view of the thematic development of children's literature across centuries.

Sentiment analysis

Sentiment analysis evaluates whether a sentence or paragraph is positive, negative or neutral, making it an invaluable tool either used alone or when paired with other DH techniques. In the case of the word 'hand', for example, sentiment analysis can reveal the emotional context in which the word is used. It can also explore how the sentiment around the word varies each time it appears, how this usage shifts and what patterns emerge throughout the text. This allows researchers to understand the emotional landscape of a word or theme in great depth.

Computational stylistics

Computational stylistics offers tools for analysing various linguistic factors, such as word categories, vocabulary level, sentence structure, syntactic information, word density, dependency parsing and more. These tools enable detailed and nuanced analysis of the formal aspects of the language, from the level of individual words to entire paragraphs. This can help identify the stylistic choices that authors make in children's literature, offering insights into their narrative techniques, language complexity and overall writing style.

Social network analysis

Social network analysis helps trace the relationships between characters within a narrative, revealing their relative importance, interactions and positioning within the social hierarchy of the story. Social network analysis can also track how these relationships evolve throughout the story, providing a dynamic view of the narrative structure and character development.

DH tools can also be used in combination, leading to more sophisticated and in-depth research questions. For example, Named Entity Recognition (NER), a mature NLP tool, can extract names of people and places from a text. This information can then be combined with sentiment analysis to examine how different characters are portrayed with varying attitudes, or how characters move between places and interact with one another. When combined with direct speech analysis, which identifies the speaker of each utterance, researchers can construct a detailed social network of interactions that evolves across the text. This multidimensional approach allows for a far richer analysis of the text than traditional methods.

The application of DH in literary studies, particularly in children's literature research, is still in its preliminary stages. These data-driven and technology-led literary research questions are innovative because they enable the exploration of entirely new questions – ones that would be impossible to address through traditional literary criticism due to their scope or complexity. For instance, previously it would have been impossible to ask how the length and frequency of direct speech have changed over the centuries, or how often and rapidly characters move between locations. Such tasks are beyond the human capacity to perform manually, but digital tools make them not only possible but also manageable.

DH-oriented research in children's literature does not aim to challenge or replace traditional methods but rather to complement and expand them. Far from diminishing the value of traditional approaches, DH tools open new avenues for research and offer scholars the chance to ask questions that would otherwise remain unanswered. By providing quantitative and qualitative analyses of texts from different angles, DH offers a richer, more comprehensive understanding of children's literature. It is also important to note that the emergence of large language models (LLMs) like ChatGPT and Claude, which have excellent programming capabilities, has made DH research more accessible than ever before. It no longer requires rigorous computer science training or years of study in programming for a scholar in children's literature to begin to engage with DH research. As a result, anyone with an interest in exploring the potential of DH in children's literature research can embark on this exciting journey, regardless of their technical background.

5.4.4 Biographical research by Michelle J. Smith

A significant amount of children's literature scholarship is interested in theoretical, critical or historical approaches to the analysis of texts for young people. Yet researchers at times require biographical information about authors, editors and illustrators, as well as details of the publishers with whom they worked. The lives of canonical authors, such as Lewis Carroll, Carlo Collodi, Astrid Lindgren and Maurice Sendak, are often the subject of widely available biographies and articles. Other authors, particularly those whose work has not such an extensive global reach, can prove more elusive and will require you to undertake some archival research to establish the basic details of their lives, careers and publication histories. You can undertake your research by thinking about both primary and secondary sources. Primary sources include contemporary newspapers and magazines, which can be located via searches in major research databases such as Gale's NewsVault, ProQuest's American Periodicals or China's Quanguo baokan suoyin (National Index to Chinese Newspapers & Periodicals). A growing number of countries have created freely accessible digital repositories of national newspapers, such as the National Library of Australia's Trove and the National Library of New Zealand's Papers Past, or full search capabilities with a limited set of digitized papers, as in the case of the Library of Congress's Chronicling America initiative. Within these newspapers and magazines, you may find articles, stories, illustrations, or other artwork contributed by the person you are researching, or articles about them or their books.

For some authors, you will be able to locate personal papers, such as diaries and notebooks, that may be housed within archives and libraries. You will usually have to travel to view these original documents in person at rare books reading rooms (see Section 5.3), although archival materials relating to major figures are increasingly being digitized. Some publishers and literary agents donate their historical correspondence files to libraries: these can provide insight into the negotiations surrounding book publication, editorial decision-making and personal issues that may have affected a writer or illustrator. For more contemporary authors, oral history recordings or television interviews can provide the author's first-hand perspective on life events. These can be found via traditional research channels, such as within the physical or digital collections of major libraries, or from television recordings hosted on websites such as YouTube.

Secondary sources include biographical dictionaries, the most notable of which are the *Oxford Dictionary of National Biography* and the *American National Biography*, though equivalent publications exist for many countries, such as the *Dictionary of Canadian Biography/Dictionnaire biographique du Canada*, *Neue Deutsche Biographie* and the *Diccionario biográfico español*. Biographical books are an obvious place to start your research for well-known authors; however, entries in literary encyclopaedias and dictionaries of artists can also provide basic and useful information for most notable figures. Newspaper searches may also locate obituaries for deceased authors and illustrators, which will include fact-checked biographical information. You can try searching for an author, illustrator or editor's name in the digital archives of major newspapers such as the *Times* or the *New York Times*.

5.4.5 Biographical research case study: Cecilia May Gibbs by Michelle J. Smith

I was invited by the *Australian Dictionary of Biography* (*ADB*) to write a new entry for the well-known Australian author, illustrator and cartoonist May Gibbs (1877–1969), who is famous for the *Snugglepot and Cuddlepie* series of books. Helpfully, she was the subject of two commercially published books, one of which focuses on her work as an artist and another on her life more generally. A range of other sources offered fresh information, particularly as the previous *ADB* entry for Gibbs was written almost fifty years ago and, reflecting the sexism of the time, was 'shared' with her lesser-known father. Digitized newspaper searches provided a way to confirm and expand upon the information contained in these secondary sources, and to access copies of her long-running comic strip, *Bib and Bub* (1924–67). Among thousands of articles relating to Gibbs was one from the *Sydney Morning Herald* in 1938 that contained her matter-of-fact thoughts about why she continued to published under her maiden name after marriage, and her opinions on what other women artists ought to do: 'if she has a striking name and he has not, then I think it would be wiser for the woman to continue using her own' (Pearson, 12).

Significant collections of Gibbs' family letters, professional papers, original manuscripts and illustrations, and personal copies of her own books are held at the State Library of New South Wales. This rich collection of primary sources offered insights into her negotiations with various book and newspaper publishers, expectations surrounding royalties and the quality of printing of her books, and details about her personal life from childhood through to her marriage in 1919. Her letters, for example, show her distress at the inferior print quality of the Gumnut Babies books after Angus & Robertson began to publish them alongside her cartoon books: 'Do not let the Babies be suffering from measles [referring to the 'spotty' image] as in the cover design of old B. and B. [*Bib and Bub*] as this is very distressing to their mother' (Walsh, 138).

Simple online searches revealed that two interviews were recorded with Gibbs in 1968, one year prior to her death, which were freely available to listen to via Trove, a repository hosted by the National Library of Australia. The same online resource also held an interview with author and illustrator of fairy characters, Pixie O'Harris (1903–91). O'Harris one of Gibbs's contemporaries, provided insight on the community between fledgling women writers and artists in the period, specifically the multiple ways that Gibbs supported O'Harris at the beginning of her career. Design and Art Australia Online provided a biography with a specialist perspective on Gibbs's drawings and sketches available in the archives, and a fuller consideration of her pioneering work as Australia's first resident, professional cartoonist.

Biographical research in archives often informs other kinds of projects, including those that span long periods, multiple kinds of materials and the lived experience of texts, as the case study below demonstrates.

5.4.6 Case study: Tracing children's books and reading culture (1750–1850) by Charlotte Appel and Nina Christensen

In a research project funded by the Danish Research Council 2016–19, we explored how a market for children's books and a cross-media and intergenerational reading culture emerged in Denmark 1750–1850. At the beginning of this period, few books were published specifically for children, mainly cathechism primers and other religious texts. Around 1850, the market for children's books flourished, resulting in a variety of genres and formats for different age groups and in different qualities and price ranges. Our initial reseach interest concerned questions such as: which books were available for children, what were the affordances and characteristics of these books, and how did children use them in practice? As a methodolocal guiding principle we aimed to 'follow the child' and 'follow the book'. In order to this, we combined quantitative and qualitative methods: we wanted to map what was actually *available* for children, but also to investigate how individual children made *use* of books in different contexts.

In Denmark, research in children's literature from this period has traditionally been based on the titles included in two subsections of the Danish national bibliography, *Bibliotheca Danica* (1872–1901), covering Danish printed materials from 1482 to 1840: 'Moralizing, didactic and entertainting redading for children' (*c.* 140 titles) and 'Primers and readers' (*c.* 110 titles). These categories were based on the old systematic library catalogues. Instead, we wanted to identify and include *all* titles published for children, not only the ones later placed in the aforementioned categories. Therefore, we based our mapping of children's books on a database consisting of all titles from *Bibliotheca Danica*, created by historian Gunnar Lind for another project, but generously shared with us. We extracted all publications from 1750–1840, and added titles from 1841–49, identified through the online database of the Royal Library, which led to a total of *c.* 56,000 titles. Now, our hunt for books published with children as an intended audience could begin. By using a number of search terms such as 'child', 'children', 'girl', 'boy', 'youth' and 'school' in booktitles, we ended up with around 4,700 hits which we inspected by reading through all titles and removing 'false hits' (books with seach terms in the title but not published for children). The result was a corpus of around 3,100 publications for children, including reprints, with great variation in genres and topics. Many titles had been 'hiding' in categories with books for (mainly) adults, such as drama, poetry and religious texts, or in categories for the natural sciences.

The next step was to inspect copies of the *books for children* we had identified. Since the project was hosted by the Royal Danish Library, we were fortunate to have our own office, classified as a 'reading room', within the library itself. This meant that we could gather a large part of our corpus on the shelves around us or, in the case of the most valuable copies, in a special safety box next to our desks. The office was rather small and dark, but it was a wonderful playground for research. Here we could examine the material qualities of specific books, as well as their texts, paratexts and illustrations.

But what about children's actual use of books? Most copies in the Royal Library had been sent directly from the printer to the library and rarely showed traces of use. Therefore, we also visited other collections in Denmark, Germany and the United States, and consulted antiquarian booksellers in order to find copies with dedications and owners' stamps, notes, drawings, and wear and tear. Private bindings also provided information on relationships between owner and book and the book as a gift or a reward.

When it comes to children's use of books in practice, children's letters and diaries were other particularly useful sources of information. The Royal Library holds a collection of letters, mainly written by persons who are considered of cultural importance, normally excluding children. In the database of letters, it is not possible to search directly for children's letters. Nevertheless, we tried to identify persons who we knew had children or possibly a special interest in children and childhood. In this way, we came across the astonishing correspondance between Ida Thiele (1830–63) and her father Just Mathias Thiele (1795–1874), beginning when Ida was around six years old and had just lost her mother. Despite the fact that the family was part of the cultural elite and befriended by figures such as H. C. Andersen, Ida only mentioned a limited number of books in her letters. Instead, she described her joy of going to the theatre, creating puppets for her own puppet theatre and creating drama performances with her cousins. Preserved letters from her young cousin reveal that they also created picturebooks for each other.

Such traces piqued our interest in children's reading culture across media and as a relational practice. At this point in the research process, we found methodological inspiration in the concepts of *media repertoires* and *media ensembles* developed by Hepp and Hasebrink (2017) and *relational agency* (Spyrou et al., 2019). In order to study how different children – with respect to gender, social status and geographical setting – were active in creating their own 'literary diet' across media, we used a wide selection of Danish autobiographies, describing childhood experiences 1750–1850, as sources (Appel, Christensen and Staffensen, 2022). This gave new insights into how children read books published for adults, created their own books and media, or co-created them with adults, alongside encountering some of the books published explicitly for them.

One outcome of our project that we think may be widely applicable is a new and broad definition of *children's reading culture* as the interplay between

- the characteristics and affordances offered by books and other media to their readers,
- the activities in which readers engage when using books and other media as their point of departure,
- the contexts (spatial, social, institutional) within which the activities take place,
- the relationships that arise from and around the use of books and other media,
- the meanings ascribed to and the experiences gained from readers' activities with books and other media.

Another result was a model showing children's reading culture as a practice across media and intended audiences, as shown in the figure below.

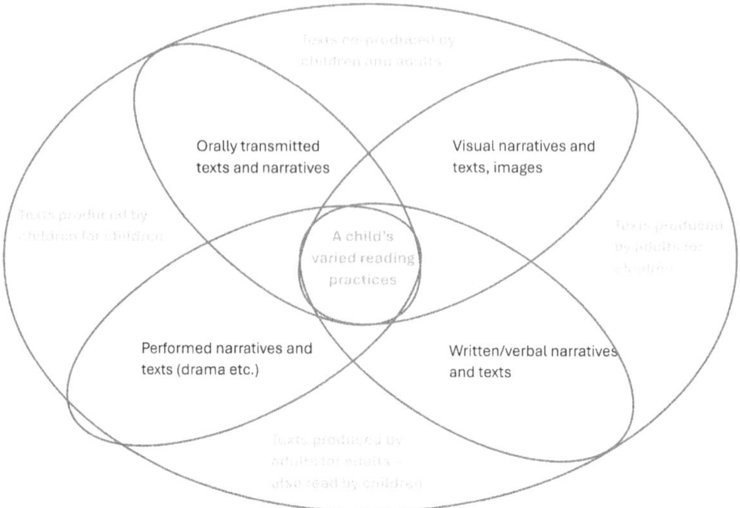

5.4.7 Using visual materials by Dafna Zur

The training of children's literary scholars usually involves a combination of literary theory and context-specific education related to the cultural and historical background of the texts under consideration. But there is one piece of education that is typically, and very critically, missing from our training: how to think and write about images. Additionally, the training literary scholars receive involves published works – magazines, books, newspapers and other print materials that made their way into public circulation by some process of consensus. When it comes to archival texts and images – and by 'archival' I mean unpublished materials that have been collected and preserved because of their documentary significance – literary training needs to be extended to account for archives' messy and contingent character. It is also important not to be too literal about the term 'archive'. For example, as well as named archives in libraries and dedicated collections, art, design and toy museums may hold sketchbooks, original illustrations, letters and other materials relevant to visual – and indeed other aspects of research into the work of authors and illustrators.

Texts for children, whether published or archival, are often accompanied by visual images. The reasons for this include the conviction that children can learn through images in the pre-literate stage and that illustrated literature can thus build early literacy; that a multi-sensory experience is better suited to children and more likely to keep them engaged, and that images help with the marketing aspects of children's literature. For these reasons, scholars of children's literature must account for visual images from the moment we begin our research journey. How, then, shall we proceed? What attention may an archival image demand?

Scholars cannot expect images to speak for themselves. Images should not be treated as decorative or marginal, just as texts cannot be treated as self-evident. Both texts and images require interpretation. Interpretation of images draws on the many methodologies made available through art theory and criticism and archival studies; some scholarship is specific to children's literature genres and formats (see further reading, below). Molly Bang's *Picture This: How Pictures Work* (1991), a book written by a picturebook artist about how artists choose colour, shape and layout to create their desired response in readers, is a helpful resource. The contingent character of archives demands additional questions: How can an image's date be determined? What does the material on which the image is printed reveal? When archival images lack an accompanying narrative, researchers must draw on the broader material, historical or literary context to interpret them, and consider why this material was preserved.

Archivists can be helpful in answering a variety of questions, but often researchers must investigate and draw on wider knowledge when using archival images. The questions we ask of images are not unlike those addressed to texts, including: What implicit/explicit understanding of the child is communicated in a given image? What medium has the artist chosen, and why? What does the image reveal about the creator's view of what children should know about the world? How does this image relate to the visual culture of its time, both for children and, equally importantly, *not* for children?

Finally, but crucially, is the image working *with* or *against* the text? Does it resist conventional interpretation?

Images can and should become part of any scholar's analytic endeavours, and we should continue producing scholarship that supports more research on visual analysis.

5.4.8 Case study: Judith Kerr's and Tomi Ungerer's Nazi-era juvenilia by Lucy Stone

I was fortunate to study the juvenilia (written and illustrated) of children's author-illustrators Judith Kerr (1923–2019) and Tomi Ungerer (1931–2019) for my PhD. Both took drawing seriously from the age of four or five and had heightened artistic faculties. Their mothers encouraged and enabled their artmaking, from their early years through the tumultuous Nazi era, when the Kerrs were forced to migrate from their Berlin home and the Ungerers' home region of Alsace was annexed to Germany. It is also largely thanks to the efforts of their mothers that their earliest drawings have survived and been conserved. Kerr's juvenilia are housed between Seven Stories, the National Centre for Children's Books, UK, and the Academy of Arts in Berlin, Germany. The majority of Ungerer's childhood drawings are held at the Tomi Ungerer Museum – International Illustration Centre in Strasbourg, France.

In this case, proficiency in English, German and French was essential for accessing and reading the archival material. The Berlin and Strasbourg databases are in German and French respectively, while many of the childhood drawings in all three collections are either captioned or illustrations of texts (manuscripts, letters, school exercise books) in one or a combination of languages. While I could manage the German, I needed to take a French reading course before I could work with the entirety of the collections. Discussions with the archivist and director (in a mixture of French and English) about my research led to invitations to contribute to museum publications and meet Tomi Ungerer; they were invaluable in developing knowledge of his creative practice, context, and even traditional Alsatian baked goods that the director kindly brought for me! The archivists at the Kerr collections were also knowledgeable and generous with their time and help. When conducting archival research, it is always worth talking with the archivists about your research and seeking advice, where possible: in my experience, I gleaned information from these conversations that I could not have found in the catalogues or materials themselves.

Being in Berlin and Strasbourg, where Kerr and Ungerer lived and drew as children, helped me contextualize their drawings, but it was sometimes overwhelming, especially in Berlin. I found myself immersed in and disorientated by multiple histories in and outside of the archive, due to the visual material of the city itself – Holocaust memorials, physical 'battle scars' on the buildings and the Kerrs' former neighbourhood. Such experiences can create a particular and productive 'affective space' for reading archival material (Tamboukou, 2017: 81), but I had to ground myself in the present again (on the emotional labour of archival research, see Hodgson, 2023).

I viewed and gathered as much material as possible on my visits (see Section 5.5.2). As I wanted to find and then explore the motifs that are prevalent across the juvenilia and adult-authored texts, I felt it necessary to look at everything. (Researchers interested in only a particular aspect of the archive and/or limited resources may choose to take a targeted approach.) I took photos of images with my phone (where permitted) and made detailed notes and some sketches with details of compositions to refer to back at my desk. I recorded bibliographic (e.g. date, title and attended addressee of composition, if provided) and iconographic (imagery) information. Although many drawings are paired with words, it was also important to record their visual elements, such as media, line, shadow, dimensions and technique (e.g. perspective; *pentimento*); essentially how the drawings' narratives are told visually rather than verbally. The physical material gave some clue to the period in which the undated drawings were composed: particular types of paper were only available to Kerr and Ungerer at certain points in their childhoods.

I included copies of seventy-eight drawings in my thesis (see Works Cited) supplied digitally by the archives or scanned reproductions from publications. While they chart the author-illustrators' development as artists and storytellers, the subject matter cannot always be read literally. Reading their drawings alongside those by other children in the Nazi era, I showed that the idyllic domestic and rural scenes are not escapes from but responses to the ways National Socialism affected their childhoods. Motifs play out in their literary and creative works across their lifetimes, but I also found that the stories of childhood displacement and war changed over time. For these reasons, juvenilia such as these comprise an important resource for scholars interested in forced migration, conflict, children's voices and kinship approaches to child- and adult-authored texts.

5.4.9 Identifying readers' responses: The case of Beverley Naidoo by Helen King

Readers' responses to literature are a valuable resource for children's literature researchers. The Beverley Naidoo collection is a good example of how responses can shed light on the reception of children's books; responses to her fiction show how her readers recognized themselves in her fiction and expressed empathy towards her characters.

Authors' archives can be a good place to locate responses, as authors often preserve materials sent to them. These materials may consist of letters, artwork, creative writing or classroom assignments, and offer insights into the social and pedagogical impact of children's books. Naidoo is a South African children's author working in the UK, best known for chapter book fiction such *Journey to Jo'burg* (1985) and *The Other Side of Truth* (2000). Naidoo's archive, held by Seven Stories, the National Centre for Children's Books, UK, is well-organized, reflective of her tendency to preserve and label everything. This is not always the case, and researchers may have to search painstakingly, and consult archive staff, when looking for readers' responses. Those in Naidoo's archive are mostly from school groups, sent by teachers, with a smaller number sent to Naidoo independently by individual readers. The preponderance of school-based responses is indicative of the fact that children are more likely to produce tangible responses in the classroom, and that teachers are more likely than are individual children to send these responses to the author in question. This is a good example of one of the central principles of reading any archival material, which is to read for what is absent as much as what is present.

When identifying readers' responses, it is important to gather as much context as possible from the archive itself. Regarding responses from schools, Naidoo often preserved the accompanying teacher's letter and her own reply alongside the children's responses. In my own research on Naidoo's work, a simple internet search often yielded additional details about the school and local context out of which these responses emerged. Commonalities between responses may also reveal how a book has been taught. For example, responses to *Journey to Jo'burg* from a Florida class in 2010 show children relating the text to their own experiences of poverty and migration, indicating that their teacher encouraged them to respond through the lens of personal experience. Paying attention to how sociocultural trends and current events shape reader responses is crucial, especially in the example above, when the readers, authors and researcher in question are situated in different international contexts.

Such readings on the individual and structural level need not be at odds with one another, nor undermine the agency of child readers. My own analysis of responses to *Journey to Jo'burg* explored how Naidoo's readers engaged with the anti-racist ideology of the text, demonstrating that the agency of these child readers emerges from their reading context, as defined by their classroom and sociocultural environment (King, 2022; 2023). Research into reader responses has particular value in light of recent turns towards participatory approaches to children's literature, as engaging with them allows researchers to place the child at the centre of literary research.

5.5 Conducting archival research

5.5.1 Protocols and etiquette by Minjie Chen

New users of special collections may find navigating their access policies and procedures daunting. Unlike open-stack libraries, special collections and archival institutions balance the need for user access and long-term preservation by storing materials in facilities closed off to the public and usually climate-controlled. Requested materials are brought to the reading room by staff for researchers. Understanding the rules will help you research without damaging items.

- Be prepared to ask clarifying questions both before your visit and while onsite (see Section 5.3), even if you have used the collection before or have experience with other archives. As memory institutions continue to embrace technological innovations, new service models and a changing environment (such as a global pandemic or cyber-attacks), users must expect shifting rules over time, and varying procedures across institutions.
- Your preparation includes checking what devices and supplies you may bring into the reading room (see Section 5.3); store other personal belongings in the locker or cloakroom provided by the institution. Special collections may mandate the use of pencils around collection materials. Food and drink are not allowed in reading rooms.
- Handle collection materials with care (see Section 5.5.4).
- Keep items and folders in the original order you receive them. If you notice any abnormalities, notify the staff and do not attempt to reorganize on your own. If a bound volume has untrimmed leaves or pages that are stuck together, always ask a staff member for help.
- Be prepared for security checks of personal items when exiting the reading room.

5.5.2 Gathering, storing and acknowledging information by Minjie Chen and Helen King

Even a veteran library user faces a learning curve when approaching a new institution's resource discovery system, and those used by special collections and archives may pose their own quirky challenges. For example, whereas online catalogues are ubiquitous in memory institutions, they represent only those resources that a library has described and indexed electronically. Print catalogues, if available onsite or even in your own institutional library, are browsable and might supplement what a special collection has made searchable online.

Additionally, archival collections are often described in guides known as 'finding aids', which record the contents of a collection hierarchically: box-by-box, folder-by-folder to illuminate the broader context and internal relationships of the items. It is searchable through a platform separate from the more familiar library catalogues, which typically describe materials title-by-title. Finally, very few online catalogues offer a reliable way of restricting a search to children's materials, either because such resources are not consistently identified as such, or a discovery system does not index this dimension. Staff members are your best resource, as they may know tips and proxies, such as location codes of a children's collection, a collector's name, or the search term 'juvenile literature', that yield more accurate and exhaustive results.

Depending on the interface of the online catalogue, you can apply the same search techniques as you would with any general library collection: snowball keywords by taking notes from relevant catalogue records you have retrieved; loosen up or tighten your search criteria through the all-cap Boolean operators of 'AND', 'OR' and less commonly, 'NOT'; and follow hyperlinked subject terms to harvest records that share the same topics or formats. Subject and genre terms are taken from controlled vocabularies and assigned to records deemed as highly relevant by human cataloguers; they can sharpen your results if a keyword search scoops up too many tangential titles.

Now that you have located your sources – after having poured over dusty volumes, scrutinized fading inscriptions and leafed through fragile sheets in a sterile reading room that is perhaps no warmer than an igloo – it is time to record and organize your data. When recording your archival findings, it is important to think about a) locating the materials in the future, and b) what information you will need when citing (see below).

Many archives allow photographs, though some charge, so make sure to ask for permission. Come prepared to use a pencil rather than pen for paper notes, as pens are generally not allowed in archive reading rooms. If possible, the best way of recording archival findings is to take notes, either digitally or on paper and then typed up, that correspond to photographs. (If photographs are not allowed, make sure your notes are detailed.) Be sure to record the date, author and catalogue location of all materials, if known.

When titling folders and files, adopt a naming scheme that allows you to identify each quickly and easily; it should also easily be cross-referenced with the archive catalogue. For good measure, use the 'Save as PDF' feature of your web browser when using an online catalogue, which helps when you need to build a citation list. Use the same naming scheme for notes and photos, and change the default names of your image files to refer to page numbers or keywords as a reminder of what has interested you. It is important to set aside time to do this as soon as possible after visiting the archive, as it can be time-consuming and will be easiest when the experience is fresh.

It is prudent to back up the electronic bytes you have painstakingly gathered. Make a copy in a second location, which can be an external hard drive or a cloud space or, given the possibility of hacks and other cloud etc failures, both: no system, plan or device is foolproof. A data storage medium can age in a limited number of years, and the backup needs to be transferred before the external drive corrupts and becomes unreadable. Check different formats to see how well they withstand migration, especially if you work with non-Roman languages. When you move a .txt file that contains Unicode characters in and out of the cloud storage, do the texts display properly or turn into gibberish?

If a folder has multiple levels of subfolders nestled, does its cloud copy keep all the files and tree structure intact?

If your primary sources contain multimedia files, it is worth investigating which formats are the most robust against digital obsolescence. A perfectly working video may suddenly become unreadable when your computer upgrades to the next operating system! Some formats, however, enjoy more longevity than others, and you may want to archive a copy that has been converted to formats that meet preservation standards. The Smithsonian Institution, for example, approves .wav for audio files and .mov and .avi for video files, among other recommended formats ('Recommended', 2017).

When citing archival materials, there are two things to bear in mind: consistency and making it easy for future researchers to find the materials you have cited. For published or unpublished texts found in the archive, and for letters or emails, you can abide by whatever citation system you are using for your bibliography (MLA, Harvard, etc.), which should always include the catalogue location. However, many items found in archives are idiosyncratic and do not fit easily into these citation systems. Examples could be unnamed photographs, or notes written on the back of an envelope. Come up with your own system of naming these items that is consistent. A good rule with any untitled text is to use the first sentence or the first few words on the page as the title. You can name things as 'untitled' or 'unnamed' when citing them, as long as there are other details that identify the item. When multiple items carry the same catalogue number, further details will be needed in your citation to identify it.

5.5.3 Recognizing/recovering unused material by Elizabeth West

When conducting archival research, the prospect of discovering an entirely new rich seam of untapped but relevant material is always the dream. It does not happen often, and that is not necessarily a problem: part of the skill of collections-based research is reinterpreting or recontextualizing an archive to bring new insights to material, regardless of how many other researchers have accessed and analysed it in the past. However, to come across a collection – whether it is simply a folder of correspondence or several boxes of files – that has not been studied before is exciting and potentially rewarding.

Of course, it might not be immediately obvious whether or not the archive in question is unused. One way to determine this is to search for citations in related publications. Alternatively, a conversation with the archivist or reading room staff is often a good way to discover whether this material has been called up recently or, indeed, ever. The accessibility of the material can also give an indication of its popularity: the collection I discuss in this case study was stored offsite and calling it up required advance notice (see Section 5.2).

5.5.4 Case study: The Williams-Ellis family and *In and Out of Doors* records by Elizabeth West

This case study uses the example of a hitherto unused collection of correspondence that I uncovered while I was researching my doctoral thesis on twentieth-century children's publishing. The main focus of my research was within the University of Reading's Archive of British Printing and Publishing, which contains the records of major British publishers including Chatto & Windus, Allen & Unwin and Routledge Kegan Paul. I carried out my initial research using the online catalogue, ordering the material I was interested in and spending days at the Reading Room. One early lesson I learnt was to think about the language of the organizations I was exploring: while my earliest searches used terms such as 'child' and 'children', in publishing terms, books for this audience were often referred to as 'juveniles'. Changing my search criteria resulted in a whole new set of records for me to investigate (see Section 5.2).

Another key lesson I learnt was that, particularly when reading correspondence, one record can lead to another, and it was just such a trail of breadcrumbs that led me to the undiscovered Williams-Ellis files. While reading correspondence within the Routledge Kegan Paul (RKP) records, I came across a discussion between pioneering children's editor, Eleanor Graham, and Thomas Ragg, a publisher at RKP. Graham was working for the Children's Book Club, a subscription service for librarians and schools in the mid-1930s. Ragg regularly discussed with Graham the books she was recommending and the books RKP were keen to have included on the list. One such book was *In and Out of Doors*, written by Amabel Williams-Ellis and her family, and edited by Ragg. Graham clearly knew and admired Williams-Ellis, and the book sounded interesting, not least because, unusually, it appeared to have been a family endeavour, so I investigated further to see what archival material existed.

It transpired that there were several folders relating to Amabel Williams-Ellis and *In and Out of Doors* within the RKP archive at Reading. They were stored offsite, and one of the reading room staff mentioned that she didn't think that they had ever been requested before. This sounded intriguing. . . . What followed was one of the most satisfying episodes of my doctoral research. Not only did I uncover a cache of incredibly rich documents which told the story of an extraordinary family but, more importantly, the material opened up new research pathways which informed and enriched my thesis in ways that I had not predicted and might not have achieved had I not followed that trail of breadcrumbs and checked out a passing reference in one letter.

Amabel Williams-Ellis was a member of the culturally and politically influential (in Britain) Strachey family. She grew up in an atmosphere of political and intellectual enquiry and, with her husband, Clough, was deeply involved in the anti-fascist movement. Williams-Ellis was a journalist, reviewer and prolific author of predominantly non-fiction books, many of which were for children. In 1937 Amabel, Clough and their three teenage children, Susan, Christopher and Charlotte, joined forces to produce *In and Out of Doors*, a 'compendium of sage advice' for children. It was a 'weekend book': an anthology that combined folk tales, poetry and prose with instructional chapters on nature, camping, sailing, first aid and cookery, alongside games, puzzles and craft activities.

Books of this kind were popular during this period, but although many were cobbled together from much-used and reprinted material, this volume was unusual in that, with the exception of the poetry and other excerpts, it was written from scratch. Amabel rewrote the folk tales, Susan provided illustrations and oversaw the overall design of the book's jacket and title pages; Charlotte contributed to the nature sections, among others; and Christopher was in charge of the games section. Clough contributed to the photography and sailing sections, which included his hand-drawn diagrams.

The archival records follow the book's progress and contain letters, drawings and page layouts. These files reveal that the three children were key decision-makers and drivers of the project; the unusual level of agency that they possessed can be explained by their parents' progressive attitudes towards education and child-rearing. The family's correspondence with Thomas Ragg tells the story of a complex process of creation and collation, control and responsibility that resulted in a book that was itself a work of creative craftsmanship. The design and content of the book was fiercely debated at every stage, and the files contain detailed and opinionated letters from Susan and Charlotte Williams-Ellis (Christopher, while clearly involved, was apparently not as moved to correspondence). For example, a handwritten letter from Susan to Ragg demonstrates the children's hands-on approach to every detail of the book's production:

> Dear Mr Ragg
>
> I just wanted to say one thing about the title page, and that is that we all think it would be much nicer if it was all in the same type including the 'BY' & also if the whole thing was shifted up to red mark on the proof.
>
> Yours, Susan (Reading, RKP 109/13, Letter from Susan Williams-Ellis to Thomas Ragg, 11/4/37)

In and Out of Doors is a rare example of a book that was not only conceived but also produced 'by the young for the young'. In being given agency to shape and create a book that they felt met their requirements, and the requirements of their contemporaries, the Williams-Ellis children were in an unusually privileged position of power. Evidence of such involvement in the publishing process is equally rare, so this archive is valuable in that it enables us to, as Karen Sánchez-Eppler describes, 'locate in the historical record the child's voice and aspirations' (2013: 174). The letters exchanged between the Williams-Ellis children and Ragg provide an unusual insight, therefore. For example, a letter discussing the layout of the contents page as shown in the figure below makes the point that, when looking at a contents page, 'one never wants to know "what is on page 50?" But always "what page is seamanship on?"' which is a good example of how a child's eye might provide an innovative approach to accepted convention. I found being able to trace the book's creation through detailed archival correspondence such as this both satisfying and valuable.

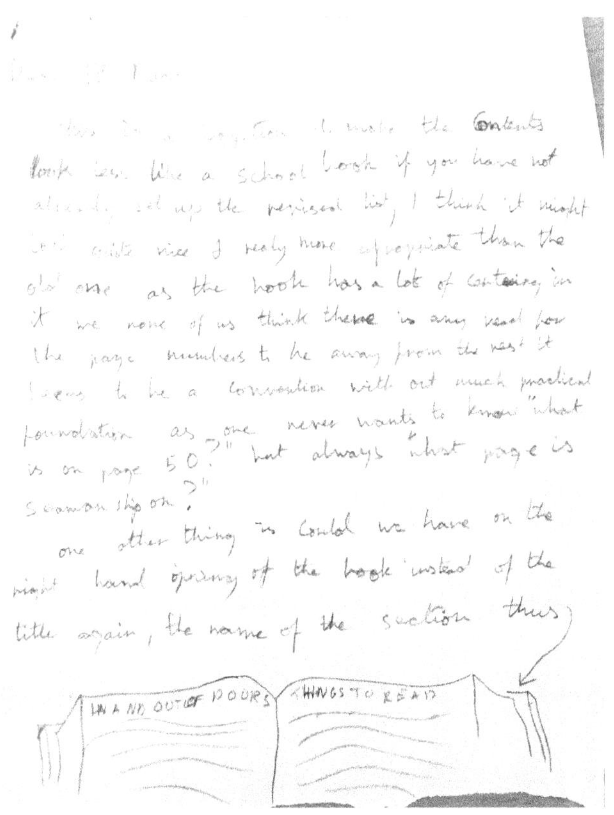

[illegible] to make the Contents look less like a School book if you have not already set up the [illegible] list, I think it might [illegible] quite nice & realy more appropriate than the old one as the book has a lot of Contains in it we none of us think there is any reasol for the page numbers to be away from the rest it seems to be a convention with out much practical foundation as one never wants to know "what is on page 50?" but always "what page is seamanship on?"

one other thing is Could we have on the right hand opening of the book instead of the title again, the name of the section thus

Conclusion

Within the context of children's literature in this period, *In and Out of Doors* occupies a liminal position at the crossroads between old and new. Its format would have been a recognizable and not particularly ground-breaking concept at the time, and much of its content is traditional; yet the book's overriding message to children – that they should be self-reliant, whatever their gender, that they should seek to find out about the world they live in and equip themselves with the skills necessary to become productive adults – makes it a worthy example of what was ideologically fresh, contemporary thinking about childhood as a construct.

The fact that it was children who were allowed to shape and create this complex project adds an extra dimension to the interest and value of this collection. Its discovery, and the accompanying investigation of a now long-forgotten book, informed a key aspect of my thesis. I was able to shape a chapter around this new primary research from deep within the archive and contextualize it within the social history of the period.

5.5.5 Working with rare and/or fragile items by Minjie Chen

Basic instructions on the proper handling of special collection materials may be available on the institutional website. Most handling techniques conform to our common sense, but it is useful to check sites nonetheless. The following are widely regarded as good practice.

- Users may be asked to wash and dry their hands before entering the reading room. Certain materials such as photographs, slides, glass plates, and metals are sensitive to human sebum and require the use of nitrile (latex-free rubber) gloves. Most items, however, may be handled with clean, gloveless hands. Contrary to popular perception, gloves are not regularly used in reading rooms, because gloved hands lose tactile sensitivity and can cause damage to pages.

- Remove personal items that may fall on or contact collection materials when you bend over the desk (e.g. ID badges, jewellery and things in shirt pockets).
- Reading rooms may provide book cradles and snake weights for gently holding a volume open without damaging its spine. Formats other than the usual bound codex – such as accordion books, scrolls, folders, prints, brittle paper, and objects – differ in form, size and condition, and may require special attention.
- Use both hands to lift objects and handle only one item at a time. Generally, only one person handles an object at a time, unless unusual formats, size or weight call for the assistance of another person.
- Hold pages and sheets at their edges to avoid touching the surface of inked areas or artworks. Do not rush; materials may be more fragile than you assume.

Table 5.2 Freely Available Websites with Digital Resources (accessed on 26 December 2023)

Collections and Archives	URL
American Antiquarian Society	http://www.americanantiquarian.org
Asian Children's Literature (National Library of Singapore)	https://www.nlb.gov.sg/main/visit-us/our-libraries-and-locations/libraries/national-library-singapore/collections/Collections/asian-children-literature
Baldwin Library of Children's Literature Digital Collection	https://baldwin.uflib.ufl.edu/
The British Library	http://www.bl.uk
Children's Book Collection at the Staatsbibliothek, Berlin	https://staatsbibliothek-berlin.de/en/about-the-library/departments/childrens-and-young-peoples-literature-department
Children's Literature Collection at Braunschweig Technische Universität	https://www.tu-braunschweig.de/en/ub/search/special-collections/childrens-book-collection
Children's Literature Collection (Roehampton University)	https://library.roehampton.ac.uk/archives/childrensliterature
Children's Literature Research Collections at the University of Minnesota	https://www.lib.umn.edu/collections/special/clrc
Digitalisierte historische Kinderbücher	http://www.bis.uni-oldenburg.de/retrodig
Find an Archive (The National Archives UK)	https://discovery.nationalarchives.gov.uk/find-an-archive
English Short Title Catalogue (ESTC)	http://estc.bl.uk
The Hockliffe Project	http://www.cts.dmu.ac.uk/hockliffe/

International Children's Digital Library	http://www.childrenslibrary.org/
International Youth Library in Munich	http://www.ijb.de/
Internet Archive	https://archive.org
Jane Johnson Manuscript Nursery Library, ca. 1740–1759 (Indiana University)	https://libraries.indiana.edu/jane-johnsons-manuscript-nursery-library
Jisc Library Hub Discover	https://discover.libraryhub.jisc.ac.uk
International Library of Children's Literature, National Diet Library, Japan	https://www.kodomo.go.jp/english/search/collection/index.html
Lindsay Shaw Children's Books (Australia)	https://www.monash.edu/library/find-and-borrow/special-collections/rare-books-two
Storyweaver (India)	https://storyweaver.org.in/en/
National Union Catalog of Manuscript Collections	http://www.loc.gov/coll/nucmc/index.html
Princeton University Library Main Catalogue	http://catalog.princeton.edu/cgi-bin/Pwebrecon.cgi?DB=local&PAGE=First
Project Gutenberg	https://www.gutenberg.org/
SurLaLune fairytales.com	http://www.surlalunefairytales.com/index.html
Toronto Public Library	http://www.torontopubliclibrary.ca/
Trove, National Library of Australia	https://trove.nla.gov.au/
WorldCat	http://www.worldcat.org/

Source: Shih-Wen Sue Chen.

Table 5.3 Subscription Databases

19th Century Masterfile™ (Paratext)
19th Century UK Periodicals (Gale/Cengage Learning)
America's Historical Newspapers (Readex)
ArchivesFinder® (Chadwyck-Healey/ProQuest)
British Newspapers 1600–1900 (Gale/Cengage Learning)
British Periodicals (ProQuest)
Early English Books Online (EEBO) (Chadwyck-Healey/ProQuest)
Eighteenth Century Collections Online (*ECCO*) (Gale/Cengage Learning)
Literature Online (Chadwyck-Healey/ProQuest)
Nineteenth-Century Short Title Catalogue (NSTC) (Chadwyck-Healey/ProQuest)

Source: Shih-Wen Sue Chen.

5.6 FURTHER READING AND RESOURCES BY SUE CHEN

Adolphs, S. (2006), *Introducing Electronic Text Analysis: A Practical Guide for Language and Literary Studies*, London: Routledge.

Adolphs, S. and D. Knight, eds (2020), *The Routledge Handbook of English Language and Digital Humanities*, London: Routledge.

Best, S. and S. Marcus (2009), 'Surface Reading: An Introduction', *Representations*, 108 (1): 1–21. https://doi.org/10.1525/rep.2009.108.1.1.

Denman-West, M. W. (1998), *Children's Literature: A Guide to Information Sources*, Englewood, Colo.: Libraries Unlimited (see Chapter 9: Special collections of children's literature).

Drucker, J. (2017), 'Why Distant Reading Isn't', *PMLA/Publications of the Modern Language Association of America*, 132 (3): 628–35. https://doi.org/10.1632/pmla.2017.132.3.628.

Giddens, E. (2017), 'Distant Reading and Children's Literature', in C. Beauvais and M. Nikolajeva (eds), *The Edinburgh Companion to Children's Literature*, 305–13, Edinburgh: Edinburgh University Press.

Griffin, M. (2018), *Once Upon a Genre: Distant Reading, the Newbery Medal, and the Affordances of Interdisciplinary Paradigms for Understanding Children's Literature*, Tampa: University of South Florida.

Hoyle, K. N. (2004), 'Libraries, Research Collections and Museums', in P. Hunt (ed.), *International Companion Encyclopedia of Children's Literature*, 2nd ed., 722–30, London: Routledge.

Jänicke, S. et al. (2015), 'On Close and Distant Reading in Digital Humanities: A Survey and Future Challenges', *EuroVis2015*: 83–103. https://diglib.eg.org/handle/10.2312/eurovisstar.20151113.083-103.

Jones, D. B. (1995), *Special Collections in Children's Literature: An International Directory*, 3rd ed., Chicago: American Library Association.

O'Sullivan, K. and P. Whyte, eds (2017), *Children's Literature Collections: Approaches to Research*, New York: Palgrave Macmillan.

Sánchez-Eppler, K. (2023), 'A World of Books: The Transnational Imagination of Child Bookmakers in Late Nineteenth-Century America', in C. Appel et al., (eds), *Transnational Books for Children: 1750–1900: Producers, Consumers, Encounters*, 356–76, Amsterdam and Philadelphia: John Benjamins.

Stover, D. (2024), 'Digital Humanities and Children's Literature', in C. Nelson et al. (eds), *The Routledge Companion to Children's Literature and Culture*, 69–79, London: Routledge.

6

Preparing material for presentations and publications, edited by Elina Druker and Kimberley Reynolds

In many countries, building an academic career in any subject area depends upon research that is recognized and validated by peer communities. Traditionally, the means for gaining these have been conference and public presentations and quality publications. While today there are more options for communicating research, these remain key activities and the skills they require can be transferred to social media and other new opportunities for raising academic research profiles.

6.1 Writing abstracts by Kimberley Reynolds

You will need to provide an abstract when responding to a call for papers (CfP), whether this is to present your research at a conference or in a book of essays. Some journals also publish abstracts at the start of articles. While each

CfP will have specific instructions that you must follow, the following advice pertains to all.

Abstracts need to convince CfP reviewers that your research is important, relevant to the topic and of high quality; also that you communicate clearly, meet deadlines and follow instructions. Conference papers are usually short: often no more than twenty minutes. Be realistic about what you can cover in twenty minutes (see Section 6.2). Focus on showing how your work opens up new ways of thinking, whether about texts, facts/data or approaches, including how your work engages with particular theoretical perspectives or theorists. Abstracts normally include keywords for use by search engines.

- Your title should capture the essence of the subject engagingly.
- Do not exceed the specified length (normally 200–300 words).
- Explain in outline what you will cover; its importance to the field and its significance to the topic of the conference or collection. This may include naming key sources.

6.1.1 Sample abstract: For a conference on 'Children's Literature, Childhood and Modernism'

'Rebuilding Britain through modernist children's books'

Keywords: British children's literature, modernism, architecture, post-war housing

Britain entered the twentieth century with an acute housing shortage. In cities, some of the nation's poorest families lived in 'one or two rooms . . . sleeping three and four to a bed with never enough chairs (or boxes) all to sit down at once' (1913 Fabian Women's Group report). Poor children in the countryside fared no better. For many children, home was far from clean, spacious or safe. It would be hard to deduce this from most children's books published in the first half of the last century, however. Popular images of home ranged from cosy cottages as pictured by Beatrix Potter and Ernest Shepard to large town houses of the kind lived in by the Banks children in P. L. Travers' *Mary Poppins* (1934). From the 1930s, a handful of left-leaning modernist writers, publishers and architects attempted both to focus attention on the urgent need for more and better housing, and to animate a discussion that was largely moribund at the level of the adult population. Their efforts took the form of books for children and young people that showed how new buildings and modernist design principles could be instrumental in positive social change. Reflecting the fact that between 1930 and 1960, 'the architecture of childhood was at the centre of architectural discourse in a way that is unique in architectural history' (Roy Kozlovsky, *The Architecture of Childhood*, 1), their books involved children in the debate about what modern houses, villages, towns and cities should and could look like. This paper will examine a selection of these texts as well as a counterblast in the form of a picturebook that examines the negative impact of suburban lifestyles on women and children. It opens up a little-known area of publishing history and shows how children's literature can influence significant social issues.

6.2 Preparing presentations

6.2.1 Content and structure by Kimberley Reynolds

Normally, conference presentations will have been preceded by the submission of an abstract which outlines what you expect to cover. This is not a straitjacket; if the work evolves in surprising ways, it is possible to adjust the content. It is important, though, to stick closely to the time you have been allocated. There are different ways to judge this: number of pages and number of words are the most common. In English, word count is very accurate: a comfortable speaking speed is 125–150 words per minute. This means, for example, a twenty-minute paper will be about 3,000 words. For audiences where English is not the first language of all the delegates, it is important to speak more slowly. It is also good to support your verbal text visually. Even if you like to speak from notes, it is helpful to draft a paper of the correct length to judge your timings. It is also good practice to rehearse it, including with any visuals you will use (Section 6.2.2).

Presentations should not be written in the same way as articles, theses or books. When listening, it is not possible to take in the same density of content, so you should avoid trying to cover too much. When it comes to presentations, less is almost always more. You should also avoid over-elaborate phrasing.

Once you have identified your most important findings in relation to the topic of the conference or other event, you need to gauge the knowledge level of your audience: do they need considerable scene-setting and context, or can you assume they start from a position similar to yours? If the latter, you can get to the heart of your findings or argument more swiftly.

Your introduction should give a clear sense of what you will cover, but without actually setting out the key sections, which is usually a deadening way to begin a presentation, and it should capture the audience's attention. Think about ways to stimulate listeners' curiosity so that they want to know about your topic and ideas. Don't undersell your work. This is your opportunity to establish the importance of what you are doing. If your audience understands the significance and value of your material from the beginning, they will be inclined to focus on what you say.

Introductions should establish the talk's trajectory. Check that the opening points firmly in the direction of your conclusion(s). Think of a presentation as a story: set out a problem, work towards a solution and provide a satisfying ending.

Illustrating your examples with images, stories and sometimes, jokes helps embed information.

Do not be afraid of humour or passion. Both can make your presentation more memorable. But be remembered for the right reasons! Always rehearse, and if you can, record and listen to yourself so you can see whether your structure works and your content is clear and compelling. You can also learn from successful speakers such as those giving public lectures and TED talks (www.ted.com).

6.2.2 Effective use of visual material by Philip Nel

In presentations, images should tell a story that illuminates your key ideas, with each slide complementing your spoken text, not necessarily by repeating it. Slides can range from maximalist to minimalist: you may want to include some of each type, both to vary the pacing and because minimalist ones are easier to create. The minimalist style highlights or summarizes a phrase, single word or concept from your text. As you speak it, the phrase – in a large typeface – appears in the centre of the screen. Be sure to use colour combinations that create maximum contrast between type and background, and avoid contrasts that would be invisible to the colour-blind: red-green and blue-yellow (see Section 4.4).

Maximalist does *not* mean cramming the slide as full as you can. Maximalist means that you design the space to make full use of its four quadrants. In a recent presentation, to suggest the influence of minstrel songs on childhood culture, I noted that 'Zip-a-dee-doo-dah' – Uncle Remus' signature song from *Song of the South* – became a pop standard, appearing on the debut albums of the Jackson 5 and Dionne Warwick. My accompanying slide used the left half of the screen for the Jackson 5's album cover, and the right half for Warwick's.

Timed animations that appear as you are making a point can be highly effective. If you want to do this, build the slide backwards: create the final version of the slide and then decide which elements you want to fade in and when. In my case, the first phase was the Jackson 5's album cover and the year 1969 below. Half a second later, Dionne Warwick's album cover appeared with the year 1963 below. Since both albums featured 'Zip-a-dee-doo-dah' on their covers, I created arrows pointing at the song title on each album. I used a timed 'fly in' for each, so the arrows arrived from off-screen and stopped when they reached the title.

You can be very particular with your slides, but the effect must not look fussy – slides should complement your words, not distract from them. Here are some general principles.

- Unless your narrative calls for something different, use a simple fade to transition between slides.
- Use maximum contrast between text and background. If your type is on a photo, you may need to alter the background of the text box. The easiest way in PowerPoint is: (1) choose the thickest border for the quotation; (2) for the text box's border and background, select 'more fill colors'.
- Sans-serif type is easier to read on a computer screen; if your presentation will be viewed via Zoom or similar, use sans serif throughout. On larger screens, typefaces with serifs can also be fine. Indeed, to evoke the typically serif'd type in a book, I sometimes use serif'd text for a quotation from a book, and then sans serif for the citation.
- Minimize screen clutter by limiting your citation to the author, title, year.
- Use content warnings. For in-person talks, the title slide should indicate that the presentation contains images of, for example, racism or trauma. For online talks, *also* announce potentially problematic content before each image and indicate when it is gone as people viewing online may join late or not have full control of their environment. Never linger on these images. Show them just long enough for people to see them and for you to say anything that requires their continued presence. Then, take them down or use a blank slide.
- For online presentations, avoid animations and ask the host where your face will appear in the broadcast. If the presenter's face appears in the top right-hand corner of your image, then leave that corner blank.

- Finally, make available an accessibility copy for audiences with disabilities (see Section 4.4). Include the full text of your talk and add descriptions of any slides that depart from your spoken text.

For print, there are four key questions: (1) How necessary is this image to your argument? (2) How easy or difficult is it to gain rights to reproduce the image (including cost) (see Section 6.3)? (3) Do you have the resources (time, money) to gain those rights? (4) How much space does the publication allow for images?

Presentations and publications can deploy a narrative art to analyse narrative art. Much of children's culture is visual; our scholarship can be visual, too.

6.2.3 Delivering your presentation by Kimberley Reynolds

The keys to successful delivery of a presentation are gauging and engaging the audience. This work starts with the submission of the abstract, when you choose your subject for the audience you anticipate, and continues through the delivery. Effective delivery depends on getting the level of content, the speed of delivery (Section 6.2.1), the supporting visuals and the engagement with your audience right. Presentations are often hybrid, with people attending in person and online, making it is almost impossible to judge how well your material is working with the whole audience, so it is advisable to seek advice about levels from the organizers at an early stage.

When speaking, do not bury your head in a script; know your material sufficiently well that you can make eye contact and judge whether you are being understood. Audiences particularly enjoy those who speak from notes rather than reading a script, but this can pose challenges for timing and for less confident speakers. Whether printed or on a screen, scripts/notes should be in a large, well-spaced font.

If you have misjudged your audience when preparing your presentation, it is possible to make adjustments while you are speaking. This may involve explaining terms and concepts that seem to be too sophisticated, adding detail and complexity if you have underestimated the audience's ability, or incorporating spontaneous elements such as jokes or anecdotes. Such modifications cannot add to length; if used, material must be cut as you go along. This means knowing your text and visuals extremely well, especially if the talk is not in your first language or is being simultaneously translated.

Presentations delivered with accompanying translation(s) require extra thought. In some cases, the translation will be done in advance, meaning you will have to submit your paper in advance and your ability to improvise will be limited. You can, though, speak close to your normal rate: slower is better for translators and for participants who are listening in what is not their first language. Live rather than prepared translation requires you to speak slowly in discrete sections of text. This doubles the amount of time it takes to deliver a presentation, so adjust your material accordingly. Visuals can be very helpful in supporting your content, but slides should not be too text-rich, as audiences need time to take in the information they contain.

It is advisable to have several versions of your presentation, including on a USB stick, in a cloud, in your email and sent to the organizers in advance, in case one is faulty or incompatible with the projection systems at the venue. This is a common problem, so try to upload and test the presentation in advance. For an online or hybrid presentation, ask your host for a short rehearsal meeting.

Presentations are performances. Body language and behaviour affect reception, so smile, try to relax (take some deep, slow breaths before you begin) and be conscious of distracting mannerisms such as waving your hands about, fidgeting or repeated throat clearing.

6.3 Copyrights and permissions for published work by Philip Nel and Elina Druker

As scholars, we may think: *art reproduced in a scholarly context should be fair use, available without a fee!* Unsurprisingly, rights-holders often disagree. But don't let this disagreement deter you from including art or quotations in your scholarship.

In the United States, works published over ninety-five years ago are now in the public domain. Works created on or after 1 January 1978 remain under copyright until seventy years after the author's/artist's death – or, if jointly created, the last surviving author's death. The seventy-year-principle also applies in the EU. However, intellectual property rights depend on national laws, so you should always make sure to follow the copyright laws in your particular country.

That said, not everything requires permission. Stills from a film can be used *gratis*. 'Orphan works', meaning works whose rights-holders are unknown or difficult to determine, can also be reproduced *gratis*, but you need to prove the status. So, keep records of your efforts to locate the owner: the 'paper trail' is your proof. To prove orphan status or locate the owner, seek advice from librarians and from those who have worked on similar material. In the process, you will learn useful information about copyright law and related areas such as corporate histories (who owns the now-defunct company that published this?) and rights-granting agencies, such as the Artists Rights Society for fine art or PLSclear (http://plsclear.com) for British publishers. Also, some institutions and archives have collections of public domain images available for use in scholarly publications.

Poetry and song lyrics pose a particular challenge. Quoting 10 per cent (or less) of a work falls under Fair Use, meaning no permission or fee is required, but limits the amount of quoted material you can include in a close reading. For instance, if you quote four lines of a sixteen-line poem, that is a full 25 per cent of the work. You must decide whether to use less direct quotation, rely more heavily on paraphrase, or pay for rights to use more of a work.

Be polite and persistent. If the online form doesn't yield results within a week, revisit the website: Is there another route to purse? If you can't find one, then find a phone number, and call. Succinctly explain what you seek – the rights to reproduce item X in publication Y. Whom should you contact? Or what advice can they give?

Since copyright laws vary in different parts of the world, learn the rules and customs in your specific country. For example, regulations concerning moral rights – the rights of an artist to claim authorship and to protect the integrity of the work – differ globally. In the United States, the law focuses more on ensuring that rights-holders profit from a work, while in most European countries, the regulations protect the creator's right to control how the work is used. This means that, in a European context, it is often the artist or their estate that should be contacted for permission. This can often be done directly via the artist's web page, through the publisher, or an agency such as the Artists Rights Society.

When you find the rights-holder or their representative, they will have questions for you. World rights or just rights for specific countries? How many print copies? How many digital copies? Publisher? They may also ask for the size of reproduction (full/half/quarter page) or the context in which the art will appear. Sometimes, the rights-holder will ask you to make a change – which can be as small as changing 'cartoon' to 'drawing' but might be more substantial. Make sure to mention if the image will be published in a publication that is Open Access, meaning it is free for all to use (for a good explanation see https://www.openaccess.nl/en/what-is-open-access#:~:text). Open Access publications will need to include this statement to confirm permission from the copyright owner or information of the original source of the image.

You may also have questions for the rights-holder. There are often academic rates for publishing an illustration, but the rights-holder may not advertise that fact. So, ask. And be willing to negotiate. 'Would it be possible to offer an academic rate for this, which will be published in journal X, a scholarly publication whose only payment is the honour of appearing within its pages?' You might directly express your own financial limits: 'As a graduate student, I unfortunately can't afford $500, but I could manage $150. Would that be possible?' Even if the result is a reduction rather than your full amount, that is a win.

Often, permission grantors will request a complimentary copy (or copies) of the publication; ask your publisher *in advance* to provide these at no cost to you (the author).

Once a work is out of print, rights typically revert to the author/artist or the estate. If the work is in print and the publisher is charging too much, you might also contact the work's creator directly – if that person is alive. Have they (unpublished) draft artwork you might use? Creators may be delighted by the scholarly interest and happy to accede to your request.

In addition to illustrating your argument, a few well-placed images or quotations in your article or book offer readers a welcome change of pace, as they pause to consider the images or words. Gaining rights to use these materials may require work, but it is worth the effort.

6.4 Submitting articles to journals by Kimberley Reynolds

Publishing articles in journals calls attention to your research; journal articles are often the first and most reliable indicators of new thinking and discoveries in a field. In the arts and humanities, institutions and funding bodies may give more weight to monographs, but journals offer more rapid and wide-ranging impact (Chapter 7). When you have a strong, discrete body of information and a compelling sense of why it is important, it is often advisable to produce an article. (If you are writing a dissertation or thesis, consult your supervisor about whether this would jeopardize your chances of completing on time – the reviewing process can be very protracted.) You can submit an article based on material that will form part of a longer work, though you must acknowledge any prior publication.

Journals are highly selective, so do your homework. Look through a range of journals to see which is most likely to accept and effectively showcase your research. This will be a journal that already publishes the kind of paper you intend to write. Because children's literature interfaces with multiple disciplines, a children's literature journal may not be the only forum. Your work might sit better in a journal of translation, linguistics, pedagogy, fine art, the history of publishing and so on. One of my most cited articles (co-authored with Schofield et al., 2019), about an augmented reality project based on David Almond's work, appeared in a publication on designing interactive systems. Other factors that will also affect your choice of journal include:

- language(s) of publication
- academic status and impact (see Chapter 7)
- article length
- ease and cost of including illustrations
- likelihood of acceptance: the higher the status, the more competitive it will be

Acceptance depends on your article being thoroughly researched and evidenced, carefully written, and presented according to the journal's house style as set out in the journal and on its website. Pay attention to the maximum length, how many and what kind of images you can include, the referencing system and details of layout. You may need to provide an abstract and some keywords (used by search engines so important for making your work visible). Use examples from the publication as models for abstracts, keywords and a biographical statement, if one is needed.

When submitting (only submit to one journal at a time), include a letter explaining why your article will interest the publication's readers and details of any ethical approval required. If the editor is interested, your article will be sent to peer reviewers who will assess its relevance, contribution to knowledge, depth of research, research methods and clarity of expression. Reviewers will recommend that it be rejected, accepted, accepted with minor changes or should be reconsidered after more substantial revisions. Any changes required will be explained. If you agree with the recommendations, resubmit the revised article with a letter explaining how you have responded to the reviewers. The final decision is usually made by the editor, though reviewers may be asked to have a second look.

6.5 Writing book chapters for an edited collection by Andrea Mei-Ying Wu and Elina Druker

Writing a book chapter for an edited volume serves several important purposes, and the specific goals will vary based on the type and scope of the edited book, as well as the editors' perspectives and objectives. Unlike monographs, edited collections consist of compiled works by several scholars around a unifying topic or research theme. Publishing a paper in a peer-reviewed journal can carry more weight compared to a book chapter. However, this may vary depending on the topic or the reputation of the publisher. Also, there are several benefits associated with writing a chapter in an edited volume on a specific theme since it puts you in context with other colleagues in a certain field of research. It can be rewarding to contribute to a book on a certain subject rather than publishing in a journal where yours may be the only article on a given subject. In an edited volume, your chapter will be in dialogue with the other chapters and together they can consolidate a body of thinking and open up a new area of research significantly. Writing a chapter in an edited collection can thus be a good way to develop your skills in writing different types of research texts and can strengthen your confidence as an author.

When preparing to write a book chapter – or even the abstract for one – it is important to bear in mind the following.

Title: an appropriate chapter title serves as a guide for readers and encapsulates the essence of the content. Ideally, a title will reflect the main theme or content of the chapter, providing a clear idea of what to expect. Consider incorporating keywords or key phrases related to the chapter's topic. This can usefully connect your chapter with the overarching theme or message of the book. Don't be afraid to revise the title as your writing progresses. Sometimes, the perfect title becomes apparent as you develop the content.

Structure: as with any piece of writing, cohesiveness and appeal require meticulous attention to structure. One effective method for achieving this is to begin by crafting a comprehensive outline that considers the theoretical and/or conceptual frameworks guiding your arguments. Identify key points, arguments and supporting details for inclusion (see Section 2.4).

Typically, a book chapter comprises an introduction, main body and conclusion, supplemented by notes and references. In the introduction, it is best to offer a succinct overview of the chapter's coverage and clearly articulate the main idea or thesis. Another effective strategy is to start with an anecdote or epigraph which carries or indicates the central message or argument intended for presentation.

In the main body, you will methodically construct and develop your arguments. A helpful strategy is to break down the chapter into manageable sections with clear headings and subheadings. This aids readers in navigating the content and comprehending the trajectory of your ideas. For instance, consider the chapter 'The (Silent) Archival Stories of Children's Literature: Munro Leaf, Cultural Tours, and the Formation of Childhood Discourse in 1960s Asia' in the book *Silence and Silencing in Children's Literature* (2021), edited by Elina Druker, Björn Sundmark, Åsa Warnqvist and Mia Österlund. The chapter comprises an introduction and four subsections with concise headings: 'Archive Study: Theoretical Considerations', 'Archival Traces: Itineraries', 'Leaf's "Nickle" Words and "Chalk Talks"' and 'Ferdinand the Silent/Silenced', followed by a conclusion. The headings encapsulate the primary theme or content of the sections, providing readers with a clear preview of what to anticipate.

Writing: your structure should be supported by writing that employs signposting (words and phrases that construct a roadmap for the ideas in your chapter and prepare readers for your conclusions) and clear transitions to ensure a seamless flow between points. The goal is to maintain coherence and avoid abrupt shifts between topics. Each point should be supported with evidence, examples or pertinent information.

Successful submission: Crafting a book chapter can prove challenging. Here are some guidelines to sidestep potential pitfalls.

Mind the word limit: edited books are usually constrained by strict word limits. The word limit for a chapter in an edited book typically falls within the range of 5,000 to 7,500 words, varying according to the publisher's specifications. Overlength chapters will be returned for cuts, or may even be rejected, so be realistic about how much you can cover in a single chapter.

Maintain a consistent format and style: steer clear of overly complex language or unexplained jargon. Depending on the academic field, humanities and social sciences commonly use the style and citation guidelines set out by MLA, APA or what is known as Chicago Style for research publications. Make sure to follow the specific style requirements for your book as stated by your publisher and ensure uniformity throughout.

Allocate time for editing and revision: successful book chapter writing demands a dedicated phase of revision and editing. This is particularly crucial if your chapter originates from a manuscript used for a conference presentation. Take the necessary time to meticulously edit and refine your chapter.

Meet your deadlines: since there are several scholars involved in an edited collection, it is important to keep to your deadlines, as delays can affect the entire editing process or result in rejection. You should always inform the editors well in advance if you know you cannot meet a deadline. Often you can negotiate a modest extension, but they need to plan for these. Once you have submitted your chapter, you may receive feedback from the editors and another deadline for returning the revised text. It is equally important to stick to this agreed deadline. If the edited collection is peer reviewed, both the proposal and the manuscript will be read by anonymous expert reviewers. This will result in more feedback. Depending on the publisher, it is not unusual for the entire process of publishing an edited collection to take up to 18–24 months.

After receiving comments and suggestions from the reviewers, you will be given some time to respond to the comments and to revise and edit your text. Make sure that you take the criticism on board and address it when revising your chapter. There might be suggestions with which you disagree. Explain to the editors why you oppose these points and ask for their advice in the situation.

When the text has been revised and accepted by the editors, you will usually receive two sets of page proofs. At the first correction stage, you will be asked to read through the text and insert any typesetting corrections or other minor changes. Make sure to read through your text carefully; mistakes can creep in during typesetting and copyediting. It is usually the editors who are responsible for gathering the responses to and corrections on the first proofs from the contributors; editors also submit the material to the publisher. In the second round, you – and/or the editors – will get a chance to check the corrections that have been made.

6.6 Writing book proposals for monographs by Bettina Kümmerling-Meibauer, Lisa Sainsbury and Lynne Vallone

Whether to launch an academic career with a monograph or a collection is a question that concerns many early career researchers (ECRs). Both options have advantages; the ultimate decision depends on several factors. If the aim is to publish a doctoral thesis or an academic study based on a research project, this should be prioritized. Moreover, most international academic communities value monographs over edited collections, often in connection with complex evaluation systems. For example, in the arts and humanities, a peer-reviewed monograph is required for tenure track or equivalent positions in the United States and the Research Excellence Framework (REF) in the United Kingdom (several other countries, including Australia and South Africa, operate similar systems, though with slightly different criteria). Consequently, this section focuses on preparing monograph proposals. Nonetheless, editing a collection also has advantages, as it boosts academic exchange with other scholars – as potential contributors – and serves as an initiation into the responsible task of editorship, which is another essential part of ECRs' publishing career.

6.6.1 Book proposals: An overview

Before submitting a book proposal, investigate potential presses to find out whether the monograph complements their lists. Many publishers include multiple book series that set different priorities with respect to theoretical approaches and thematic foci. A perusal of titles published within specific series offers insight into their overarching aims and topics prioritized. Some series do not accept doctoral theses and will reject these as a matter of course. Also consider publishers' willingness to include illustrations and the likely costs; this is particularly relevant in book projects dealing with multimodal texts.

A common concern for ECRs is whether to send book proposals to multiple presses simultaneously. Most publishers pose this question on their proposal forms, and it should be answered truthfully to avoid misunderstandings and discord. Since publishers spend considerable time identifying suitable external reviewers for proposals – ranging from two to four reviewers – they usually expect that ECRs have sent the proposal exclusively to them. Therefore, it is advisable to submit proposals to one publisher identified as the most suitable for the current project.

The aim of the book proposal is to stimulate enough interest that it will be pursued as an addition to the press's list. A proposal is particularly promising if it demonstrates the author's knowledge of current debates in the field in addition to opening new vistas on under-researched topics. Although publishers and book series editors are interested in proposals on topical issues, ECRs should avoid paying lip service to trends in order to promote their book projects, since this can be at the expense of the proposal's authenticity. A sample (Box 6.1) based on a successful proposal is provided at the end of this section.

6.6.2 Proposal submission and key features

When submitting a doctoral thesis for publication, it is important to adapt and revise it for the publication market; developing a thesis for examination is different from preparing it for a wide readership. These questions serve as a guideline when writing a proposal:

- What makes this book distinctive and commercially viable?
- Why is a new book needed, and how is the author qualified to write it?
- What will readers gain from the book?
- How does the proposed book fit into a book series or a publisher's general list?

Submit the proposal electronically as an email attachment in accordance with submission guidelines on the publisher's website. Set up the proposal through an email that serves as a covering letter, in which authors should introduce themselves and their project, highlighting the book's unique argument and indicating any portions of the work already published. Include an updated curriculum vitae as a separate attachment within the same email, unless the publisher asks that credentials be provided within the covering letter.

Typical components of proposal submissions:

- overview of the book's thesis, aims and scope, making the case for the book's importance and future impact;
- table of contents including brief descriptions of each chapter;
- explanation of how the work relates to competing books on the same topic and suggestions for ways to market the work in academic or general readership contexts;
- indication of illustrations or special figures required;
- practical matters such as length (typically expressed in word count), status of the project's degree of completion, a reasonable timetable for completion and potential reviewers.

While these elements contribute to the proposal's persuasive aim, the importance of setting out the book's argument, contexts and contribution to the field in clear, concise and dynamic prose cannot be overstated. Use the proposal's opening to grab the editor's attention through a thoughtful summary of the manuscript's rationale, intellectual contributions and unique selling points. Keep in mind that acquisitions editors are not field specialists: describe the project's relevance in jargon-free, lively prose.

The table of contents and brief chapter summaries – typically one paragraph per chapter – provide a roadmap to the work. Include the core argument for each chapter, linking the ideas from one to the next so that the book's overall claims are clearly delineated, yet avoid cluttering the summaries with too many details.

Publishers need convincing that a proposed monograph will attract readers. Key actions will help to explain who might read the book and why:

- positioning of work in a wider field;
- identifying contribution to knowledge and gap in the market;
- pinpointing market and potential readers.

Establish how arguments contribute to the field generally or to a series published by the press. Be specific here, providing titles, presses and dates of publication when referring to others' work. An annotated list of 5–10 relevant works will determine what those texts achieve and how the proposed monograph builds on them, or how it fills gaps they have left. Be mindful that authors under discussion might be called upon to review the proposal. Avoid stating that nobody has written a similar book, as misguided claims for originality risk isolating the project, implying that there is not a market for it. Reference to regional patterns and statistics helps to create a market model, identifying:

- associated disciplines, such as ecocriticism, linguistics or education;
- relevant national and international programmes of study, such as BA/MA degrees in children's literature;
- statistics confirming the growth of disciplines/programmes relevant to the field;

- audience level: undergraduate, postgraduate or established scholars;
- potential markets outside of academia, such as mainstream readerships for popular histories or biographies.

Indicate any illustrations or special figures the book requires in terms of number, status (public domain or under copyright) and reproduction value (colour or black and white). All images and figures, including tables or diagrams, should be listed/numbered on submission. It is the author's responsibility to secure permission to use images in copyright/outside of fair usage (Section 6.3). This can be a lengthy and costly process, as it can be unclear who holds rights and some are expensive (authors must cover these costs, unless contracts state otherwise). Build the permissions process into completion timelines, as they should be confirmed prior to manuscript submission.

Accurately state the project's degree of completion, date of completion if currently unfinished and anticipated word count. Deadlines for manuscript delivery should be realistic, factoring in existing commitments. It might be possible to renegotiate deadlines, but always advise publishers of potential delays as soon as possible. Deadline changes impact on the wider production team and could disrupt publication schedules.

Many publishers ask for potential manuscript reviewers, which could be for anonymous peer review, citations for marketing or book reviews. Be ambitious and list established scholars who might be interested in the monograph – there is no need to seek permission for this, as requests and payment for such work will be handled by publishers.

Follow to the letter any requirements provided by the publisher's acquisitions department. Do not include any attachments not mentioned in the guidelines for prospective authors and never underestimate the importance of proofreading proposals. A casual approach to editing and presenting proposals undermines their authority and the valuable ideas they contain.

BOX 6.1 WRITING BOOK PROPOSALS BY CATHERINE BUTLER

IT HAS BEEN SAID THAT writing a book is like setting sail in a boat you have not yet finished building. The journey from 'no book at all' to 'finished book' is a long one, with many doublings back and diversions, and not a few dead ends. At what point should the formal proposal make its appearance?

By the time I write a proposal, much thinking and reading have taken place, but relatively little connected writing. Ideas have begun to coalesce, but the details are vague. It is unclear which topics will assume the greatest importance, which may disappear altogether, and what might be the best running order.

The eventual contents page of what became *British Children's Literature in Japanese Culture* looks like this:

Introduction: Writing from the outside in

1 Wonderland or Looking-Glass? Meiji Japan through the lens of children's literature
2 Britain and the origins of Japanese children's literature
3 Canons to the West, Canons to the East: British children's books in Japan
4 Hayao Miyazaki and British children's literature
5 Children's literature, tourism and the Japanese imagination

Postscript: Reading from the inside out

Clearly, some things have changed, while others have survived more or less as planned.

The Introduction, as well as providing an outline of the book, was intended to address my position as a non-Japanese author engaging with Japanese culture. How would I deal with my own cultural and linguistic limitations? My possible (inevitable!) prejudices and assumptions? However, researching this subject led me to discover both the long cultural history of those assumptions and how deeply influenced they were by images drawn from children's literature, a frequent reference for Victorian visitors to Japan. In the end, what had been envisaged as a short historical digression swelled to become the new-minted Chapter 1.

Chapter 2 was another unanticipated addition. I had always intended to describe the introduction of British children's books to Japan over the century from the 1868 Meiji Restoration, but I originally planned to do so in the context of a wider discussion of canon formation, influence and adaptation. However, the historical story was such a fascinating and complex one, peopled by important but little-known (in the West) figures that it demanded its own chapter.

Two other chapters – those on Hayao Miyazaki and Japanese tourism – survived more or less intact. (The latter was the only one that had already been substantially written by the time the proposal was submitted.) However, much of the historical material meant for the chapters titled 'Canons to the West, Canons to the East' and 'Influence, Imitation and Reinvention' had now migrated to Chapter 2, so I merged their discussions of canon formation and influence to create a more theoretical chapter illustrated with case studies – what is now Chapter 3.

The published book is recognizable as the one in my proposal, but its changes are far from superficial. I believe they are for the better.

6.7 Blogging: Three case studies

In these three case studies, we draw on our experiences of blogging to show how to find and use your voice, and demonstrate how blogging can be a path to employment.

6.7.1 Case study 1: Blogging and non-fiction writing by Clémentine Beauvais

I began blogging about children's literature in French while doing my master's degree in 2009–10 in order to share the bits of children's literature theory and criticism that fascinated me the most. Then, blogs were a much more powerful platform for children's literature than social media, and they were especially read by teachers, librarians and parents looking for book recommendations. My blog was quite different from what was on offer in the French-speaking world, however, as it did not so much recommend children's books as offer ways to analyse and theorize them.

Initially, I didn't think about whether the material I was posting about was 'difficult' to understand; looking back, I made many assumptions about my readers' background knowledge when posting about complex theories and concepts. However, I was immediately struck by just how curious people were about those theoretical and critical insights, even if (or maybe because) they were not easy to grasp. To me, this should be the main takeaway message for anyone reaching out through blogging or social media (see Section 6.8): people on the internet are able and willing to engage with sophisticated content. There are rules you sometimes read online about blogging – that you should always connect abstract ideas to personal anecdotes, that it's always better to start with concrete examples, use analogies, avoid jargon and have a cheerful, 'engaging' voice. In my experience, these rules can all be broken. The most important, to me, is: Quality Content Not Dumbed Down.

My most successful posts have been the ones that present ideas that no one else on the internet has presented before. If I take, say, Marah Gubar's kinship theory and explain it to a French audience, I don't actually need to add lots of exclamation marks, 'hey you guys I have a personal life story that relates to this', and funny GIFs. Just by virtue of being new to almost everyone who will stumble upon my blog, it will be interesting, because it is an interesting theory.

I am not saying that writing style isn't important: it is, in fact, crucial to craft a blogging (or social media) voice that works for you and for your audience, but it is also hard to know in advance what voice that will be, because that depends on you and on your audience. I sometimes fear that well-intentioned blog posts about writing blog posts are only contributing to a standardized blog-post voice – typically ecstatic, friendly, intimate, etc. – which is more likely to lose your blog in a tide of similar ones, instead of setting it apart. This is especially true in a ChatGPT era.

While voice is essential, it is one of those things that gets fine-tuned over years and also changes – I no longer write like I did when I was twenty-one, because I have become slightly more boring, slightly less reckless but hopefully also kinder, and my voice reflects that. Content, however, remains key. A blog about lost silent films of the 1920s will always find an audience, even if the voice is only OK; a blog about writing YA literature that only recycles usual content about NaNoWriMo and creating awesome kick-ass heroines will need a really brilliant voice to stand out, because everyone who's even vaguely interested has read about that a million times.

I no longer blog as much as I used to because life gets in the way, but very many of my past blog posts have found their way into published works of non-fiction on children's literature. I have written two books on writing for children and reading children's literature, one in English and one in French, and one book on reading for pleasure, and those works would have been unthinkable without previous experience of writing for a general audience on the internet. Blogging also gave me the confidence to say to a publisher: 'I know people will want to read this, and will be able to read it; please don't make me dumb it down'. People are thirsty for quality, complex and unique knowledge, so if you start blogging or sharing your research on social media, focus on that.

6.7.2 Case study 2: Find your voice and use it by Philip Nel

As is true of Clémentine, the demands of life have dramatically slowed the frequency of my blogging. But I still blog, and I recommend blogging (or starting a Substack, which has become a popular, blog-adjacent form of self-publishing), for some of the same reasons that she does. Sometimes my blog pieces have later appeared in 'real' publications, but that is not a given.

Blogging will, however, help you develop the skills to write for a broader public. The immediacy of blogging sharpens attention, and the potentially broad audience compels you to sharpen your prose. You need to be as precise, concise and jargon-free as you can. Despite the evidence of much academic writing, complex ideas can be expressed clearly.

Because a blog post feels less formal than scholarship, blogging can also help you find your voice as a scholar. The voice I developed on the blog has carried over into my scholarship and made me a better writer. Indeed, the distinction between blogging and scholarly writing – a distinction I was conscious of when I began my blog in 2011 – has since melted away.

I admire scholars – Ebony Elizabeth Thomas and Christina Sharpe, to name but two – who elegantly weave the personal into their scholarship. While I don't expect to achieve their level of fluency any time soon, blogging has helped me figure out the role of the personal in my scholarship. Writing on my blog about the Golliwogg – a racist doll given to me by well-meaning relatives when I was a child – helped me understand how to bring my racialized experience into my work on racism in children's literature. Elements of that blog post appear in the introduction to *Was the Cat in the Hat Black?*

Since I own my blog, it is also a place where I can address subjects that my university or the state would prefer me not to discuss. Our work as scholars of children's literature is political. For example, in 2018, firearms became the leading cause of death in the United States for all children and teenagers. A dozen blog posts between 2015 and 2018 grew out of my activism against the legislature forcing 'concealed carry' onto the classrooms of Kansas universities. For me, the blog is vital because my degree of freedom of speech – another subject I've addressed on the blog – varies according to who holds political power in my state and federal governments.

The risks of blogging are not distributed equally. As a straight, cisgendered, tenured white guy, I have greater latitude to speak without fear of being attacked. Since I am a beneficiary of many unearned privileges and thus the structural oppression that sustains them, blogging is a safer space for me than it is for most people reading this paragraph. I say this not to discourage anyone, but rather to acknowledge that my subject position very much colours my assessment of the benefits of blogging.

So, weigh the risks, consider the benefits. And know that, for me, the benefits have far outweighed the risks: helping get some of the excitement of intellectual discovery onto the page, granting immediate feedback that is neither hidden by social media algorithms nor lost in the feed, and providing an efficient way to share topical information. Blogging helped me find my voice and gives me a space in which to use it.

Case study 3: Blogging and building academic-adjacent careers by Lucy Stone

Blogging played a significant role in my postgraduate journey. When I first started thinking about switching from studying medicine to children's literature, Clémentine's blog inspired me to apply for the MPhil at the University of Cambridge. At Cambridge, I contributed to the student-run blog and later established one for the Children's Literature Unit Graduate Group (CLUGG) at Newcastle University, UK, during my doctoral studies there.

Designed to foster connection between past and present CLUGG members and raise the profile of the University's Children's Literature Unit (CLU), the *Children's Literature in Newcastle* blog also taught me the basics of managing a social media site. The University's blogging service provided the platform and template (WordPress). The blog's title was selected with SEO (search engine optimization) in mind and featured an image by Judith Kerr as a nod to the CLU's close ties with Seven Stories, the National Centre for Children's Books, where Kerr's archive is held. Initially, posts appeared fortnightly during term time and covered topics such as research activities, student experience and careers. It also hosted guest contributions on related topics and provided a platform for *Refugee Tales*, broadcasting stories of indefinite immigration in the UK. Posts were disseminated via the CLUGG mailing list and the School of English's Twitter account, and data from Google Analytics provided insight into the blog's audience and reach.

My blogging experience led to academic-adjacent roles after my PhD. The experience I gained in stakeholder engagement, communications and project management transferred well to professional positions in Higher Education. In an increasingly competitive academic job market, blogging can open up alternative career pathways for researchers.

6.8 Podcasts by Katharine Capshaw, Anna Mae Duane, Victoria Ford Smith

Podcasts enable connection and collaboration. Academics often wish to create a pathway for ideas to reach a wider audience, allowing their scholarship and teaching to connect with a range of people, from fellow academics to community members to curious individuals of any background. In developing *The Children's Table* podcast, we have found success in working collaboratively and cultivating flexibility in content and mindset.

6.8.1 Designing and establishing your academic podcast

In imagining your podcast, you need a concept – one that will appeal both to your scholarly side and to a wider audience. What is distinctive about your approach? How can that particularity be broadened out, questioned, unsettled or made portable across subjects? It's a challenge to think both about your project's singular identity and how you could use that identity to touch on a range of topics, but if you wish your podcast to have legs beyond a few episodes (or seasons), you will need both a distinct identity and a broad, flexible appeal. For example, in our initial brainstorming sessions about *The Children's Table,* we focused on foregrounding the voices of children and young people throughout history. That remains a big part of our podcast's mission. For example, we featured the story of James McCune Smith, the first African American to earn an MD who, as a child and star student at the New York African Free School, met the Marquis de Lafayette, and we explored student- and community-led efforts to establish social justice-oriented curricula in schools. However, we soon decided to think about children's history writ large, to allow us more flexibility across episodes and seasons. We were eager to demonstrate a larger, central value that unites all our work: the belief that when we consider young people's participation in cultural, social and political change, it truly transforms how we understand history. That led to episodes on, for example, the persistent idea of the child as a bridge to the supernatural, from medieval Europe to colonial America to Victorian England, and another on the history of sex education in the United States.

The issue of audience is complicated for academic podcasts. As academics, we are excited about our sites of research. Will an audience be excited as well? Which audience? Many academics tend to go narrow and deep when pursuing a subject, and such an approach might not be appealing across fields. We initially hoped that *The Children's Table* would have a broad audience, from academics in various fields to parents waiting at the bus stop for their kids to get home from school. However, we found that to pitch our podcast coherently, we were inclined to speak to other academics more than to a truly wide audience. It was also important to us to respect our individual disciplinary locations and to share the conversations we have there with other scholars. From Victorian studies, to nineteenth-century American studies, to Black studies, we all contribute based on our expertise, and it is in conversation with each other that we translate the stakes of our fields. We hope that in sharing responses to key questions with each other, we are practising that translation to a wider academic audience. We found that while it is important to imagine your audience, that concept may change as you settle into your own rhythm and clarify what your unique contribution is.

Once you have determined what you want to say and to whom you want to say it, spend some time planning the nitty-gritty details of producing the podcast. Consider how you will record, edit and distribute your episodes. If you work at a college or university, your institution might have support for podcasts, including recording studios and dedicated staff members familiar with sound editing. Check with your institution's communications arm or radio station for studio space and people with editing ability. Not all institutions offer structural support for establishing and editing a podcast. In the case of *The Children's Table*, we began recording during the Covid-19 pandemic, which meant we couldn't access studio space. We sought advice from experts in our digital humanities faculty, learned about editing software and microphones through seminars and online research, and found an exceptional staff member able to help us with editing. There are several free online sources of information about every aspect of podcasting. Buzzsprout .com for instance, offers free guides and tips that are quite helpful. Creators working in languages other than English might try Spotify Podcasting, which offers support in nine languages, or Podbean, which offers eight.

Spend some time planning logistically. We purchased microphones and editing software and recorded each episode of our podcast on Zoom from our homes. We certainly had a learning curve in terms of technology, but it was exhilarating to play around with recording and to develop new competencies in partnership with others. It was satisfying to leave our comfort zones and engage in the humbling work of learning completely new skills.

A final important component of designing a podcast is planning the episodes. Most podcasts operate in terms of seasons, and each season has a focus. We found that broad concepts such as 'Spooky Children', 'School Days' and 'Secret and Hidden Childhoods' enabled us to narrow in on multiple ways to approach each topic. We decided on six one-hour (or less) episodes under each topic and use a shared Teams site to generate bare-bones scripts before recording. We alternate weeks, generating a script one week and then recording it the next. While initially we tended to write more elaborate scripts, as we gained confidence in recording and listened to early (more stilted) episodes, we were able to loosen up, both in terms of resisting the urge to write an academic paper and leaning into the lively conversation and energy around the topic we were exploring.

6.8.2 Conducting interviews

Since podcasts aim to be conversational, many involve interviews with guests. Academic interviews carry certain risks since the interviewee may not have experienced being recorded or talking informally about their subject. When you invite an interview subject to your podcast, it can be helpful to establish that you are interested in a specific compelling article or book chapter. Set that work in the context of the larger season and explain why you wish to include their perspective in the conversation. Send a set of questions ahead of time, making sure that they point the interviewee towards a discussion of the larger contributions of their work, since scholars sometimes tunnel in on specifics. Make sure to ask questions that tie the scholar's work to the big question or questions your season is exploring. Academics like to talk, and we like to listen and learn; use the questions to shape the conversation towards the imprint of your season.

6.8.3 Building an audience and managing response

When you publish an article or a book or present at a conference, you are often supported by a publisher, editors or a scholarly organization each bringing interested audiences: subscribers, for example, and conference attendees. Podcast projects typically do not enjoy those ready-made audiences, so you will need to strategize how you will get your work to the people who will be most interested in listening to it.

Begin by designing a multiplatform digital presence that makes your podcast visible and easily shareable. There is a range of easy-to-use website design platforms, such as WordPress or Wix, that will help you design a home base for your podcast's online presence. Some, such as Joomla and Smoolis, offer built-in multilingual support. Consider what you want to share in that space. Our website, for example, includes a home page that features our most recent episodes; subpages dedicated to each season and its episodes, with show notes, further reading, images and transcripts. An 'about us' page introduces our team and the podcast's purpose.

Once your website is established, you can create public accounts on major social media platforms to share updates, provide links to new episodes and invite engagement from listeners. *The Children's Table* uses Instagram, Facebook and X to tease new seasons and episodes and share particularly engaging images and sound bites. Social media posts can link back to your website and are particularly useful in spreading the word about your project; listeners can share or 'retweet' your posts to their own accounts, and you can use hashtags and links to other accounts to reach audiences adjacent to your own. Interview episodes in particular can build audiences in this way. Be sure to tag your interviewee and the press where they publish, and invite them to alert their colleagues, friends and institutional support networks so that they can circulate information about their episode.

It's useful to pair your digital presence with the promotion of your project in person – at conferences, professional events or at any venue where your listeners might convene. *The Children's Table* team presents at workshops and conferences, where we promote our work, distribute promotional materials such as stickers, and meet other podcasters to share tips and ideas.

6.8.4 Potential pitfalls

Take advantage of the audio genre and leave room for banter and conversation. Sticking too much to a script can make the episode sound more like an academic conference paper than a podcast. Since audio requires collaboration, seek out resources in your colleagues, online and at your institution. Ask questions as you go along, since this approach may be entirely new to you. Finally, give yourself some grace as you begin recording episodes. If you listen to the earliest episodes of any popular podcast, you will quickly discern how far they've come. You'll learn as you go. Don't get stymied by perfectionism.

6.9 FURTHER READING AND RESOURCES

As mentioned elsewhere in this volume, there are many excellent online resources that offer advice on academic writing and specific style guidelines. All publishers will also publish guidance on their websites. It is often useful to have general principles for good practice in one place, however, and the following are reliable sources.

Knochelmann, M. (2023), *Authorship and Publishing in the Humanities*, Cambridge: Cambridge University Press.

Harman, E. (2003), *The Thesis and the Book: A Guide for First-time Academic Authors*, Toronto: University of Toronto Press.

Hartley, J. (2008), *Academic Writing and Publishing: A Practical Handbook*, London: Routledge.

7

Funding, engagement and impact by Matthew Grenby

Teaching and research remain the cornerstones of an academic career in children's literature. But increasingly, academics – and indeed those working outside universities – are having to think about obtaining funding to pursue research and to make their research more visible and more widely relevant. Ensuring that research reaches non-academic audiences is called 'engagement'. Making sure that research brings appreciable benefits to non-academic users, whether individuals or institutions, is often called 'impact'. This chapter looks at both, but begins with some guidance on how to secure the funding that will enable you to develop and implement plans for engagement and impact.

7.1 Research funding

It is, of course, possible to produce brilliant research without obtaining special funding. Scholars working independently have sometimes been able to devote themselves to research and writing about children's literature, or to dedicate their spare time to the subject. Some of the most valuable studies and perceptive criticism in our field has been produced people working outside universities, including book collectors, librarians, journalists, teachers and children's book writers and illustrators themselves.

However, children's literature studies has steadily become more professionalized. Increasingly, it happens within universities. There are more and more opportunities for people to undertake research degrees in children's literature. Universities charge fees for anyone to take these degrees, and of course students need to be able to support themselves while they study. Some students may be able to fund their fees and living expenses themselves; for others, funding will be required, typically from a university itself, perhaps from a charity, or from a research funding agency. Equally, academics employed by universities will often have to obtain funding to undertake their research. Research may be an expectation of their job, or needed to obtain promotion. Perhaps their university will allocate a portion of their employment to research, or offer periods of leave from other duties to allow concentrated research and writing time. But often academics will want to secure additional funding to carry out particular projects, enable research trips or to pay for cover for their teaching and other duties while they think, research and write. Literary studies is, in many parts of the world, becoming more like the hard sciences, in which funding to pay for research has long been the norm. Universities are increasingly encouraging, or even requiring, their researchers to apply for and hopefully secure this external funding.

7.1.1 Postgraduate funding

Leaving aside funding from families, personal funds or private loans, there are a variety of ways in which master's and doctoral study funding is available. These are different in different parts of the world. In some countries, the majority of funding comes from universities themselves, which can offer bursaries, scholarships or fee-waivers. Generally, these are awarded on merit, but some will be aimed at specific groups of people or dedicated to specific subjects. In other countries, postgraduate degrees are government funded. Alternatively, PhD studentships may be attached to particular research projects, for which established academics have won funding. What all these schemes have in common is that candidates will need to apply for the opportunity, and that there will be many more applicants than there are places. In other words, like all research funding, they will be very competitive.

In the sciences, it is common for doctoral studentships to be offered to work on a specific, pre-defined project, with the student becoming part of a research team. This has been less common in the humanities, and in many cases, applicants are able to devise and propose their own subjects for research. If this is the case, successful applicants will have to formulate a topic that is at once original and significant, and feasible within the constraints of the resources and time available. Advice on developing a PhD proposal is given in Chapter 2. But when applying to a university for funding, you should think about more than the project itself. Consider whether the institution to which you are applying is suitable for this research. Does it have the right research environment, which might include relevant archival resources, a library with all the materials you need, any specialist equipment or suitable training and development opportunities? Does it have a flourishing cohort of students already working in your proposed area, or close ties with other disciplines besides children's literature, which will enable you to take an interdisciplinary approach? Does it have the right people in place to supervise your research? The best applications for PhD funding often focus on these 'three Ps' – Project, Place, People. If you are making a case for funding, ensuring that you address all three can help you gain a competitive edge. You might sometimes add a fourth P – Partners – since particular universities often have established relationships with other organizations that could support your research, such as a museum or library, an arts organization or heritage agency, or schools or community groups. Working with partners such as these can help you to engage people with your work, and again, if you can make this case in advance, it may give your funding application an advantage.

Indeed, in some places, PhD funding is becoming increasingly linked to collaborative opportunities. In the UK, for instance, at the time of writing, the majority of doctoral studentships in children's literature and related areas are available through a government agency called the Arts and Humanities Research Council (AHRC). The AHRC devolves its funds to universities (or consortia of universities), but in many cases those institutions or consortia will have set aside a portion of studentships for doctoral projects to be undertaken in collaboration with a non-university partner. Further, the AHRC devolves some of its funding direct to certain museums, libraries and heritage organizations, such as the British Library or the Victoria and Albert Museum, which then decide on their own priorities for research and seek universities with which to partners so that they can jointly recruit and train PhD students. Students recruited through these schemes will be jointly supervised by the university and the partner organization, and will typically spend some of their course away from the university and embedded in the non-academic organization. The aim is to give students access to materials, knowledge and expertise that would not otherwise have been available, while also providing them with opportunities to develop research that has direct impact, both on the non-academic partner and on the wider communities they can reach through that partner. This is designed to enhance the student's professional profile, giving them a route into employment. After all, less than a fifth of students who obtain a PhD in the UK obtain academic university posts after graduation. In any case, if you are applying for postdoctoral funding, it may be wise, wherever you are, to build collaborative possibilities into your application. Chapter 1 describes some of the many ways in which studying children's literature can intersect with other professions. Identifying research partners in these areas would be a good strategy both for receiving funding and making yourself employable.

7.1.2 Postdoctoral funding

The goal for many people after completing a PhD is to move into an academic job, but this can be extremely difficult. A relatively small number of universities teach children's literature, and vacancies are only seldom available. Even when jobs are advertised, competition is fierce. In many cases, experience of teaching, and perhaps engagement and impact work (see below) will be required, as well as an emerging record of publications, or even of research funding. Postdoctoral research fellowships, usually lasting one, two or three years, are an attractive proposition for those seeking to launch an academic career since they are intended to bridge the gap between PhD and a permanent university appointment, and because they allow the holder to develop a research profile.

Different schemes are on offer in different parts of the world. A famous example is the European Union's Marie Skłodowska-Curie Actions scheme, which provides funding for researchers who hold a PhD. It is entirely 'bottom-up', meaning that proposals in any scholarly field are eligible. Its distinctive feature is that it requires cross-border mobility: currently, one strand is open to researchers moving between two EU Member States (or 'Associated Countries', such as the UK, Norway, Israel or New Zealand), or coming from outside the EU/Associated country into the EU/Associated country. The second strand is for European researchers to undertake training in a non-European/non-Associated country before returning. Funding covers a living allowance, travel costs, research costs and so on, as well as providing funding to the hosting universities. Other national funders sometimes offer their own postdoctoral fellowships, often aimed exclusively at the citizens of that country. Examples include the UK's British Academy Postdoctoral Fellowships or Leverhulme Trust Early Career Fellowships, or Canada's Postdoctoral Fellowship Program. Note that some of these fellowships are open only to applicants in certain subjects.

Understandably, these fellowships are highly sought after and very competitive. The application process is onerous, and to have any chance of success, the applicant will need to have a very strong record, the application will need to be very well crafted, and the research proposal will need to be highly persuasive. Almost always, successful applications will have been co-produced by the applicant and academics in the intended host department. Indeed, as mentioned above, in some circumstances the host department will have advertised the opportunity themselves, seeking to recruit a postdoctoral researcher to help them with a pre-defined project.

7.1.2 Case study: *PiCoBoo*, a postdoctoral project by Francesca Tancini

The PiCoBoo project was funded under the European Union's Marie Skłodowska-Curie Actions programme. Its name is an abridgement of 'Picturebooks in Colour', the aim of the project being to assess the significance of nineteenth-century European picturebooks, printed in colour for children, as a catalyst for major cultural and social changes. Colour printing, which has played an important part in so many aspects of modern society and culture, had its birth in books for children. But very little work had investigated this major shift in print culture. PiCoBoo was designed, therefore, to provide the first comprehensive analysis of a large genre of books that, although mass-produced and widespread all over Europe, and of undoubted significance to the history of print as well as many individuals' reading experiences, had still been almost entirely neglected by scholarship.

At the time of the application, I had been working as a curator librarian at Italian university libraries for more than ten years. Children's book illustration was my passion, and I had been carrying out my own research activity on the subject, taking up various visiting fellowships at institutions in the United States and the United Kingdom, where Victorian-era picturebooks are held. Hoping to switch to an academic career, I applied for a Marie Skłodowska-Curie postdoctoral fellowship in 2017. The first task was to identify the best host institution: somewhere with a strong research environment in my field, and a strong supervisory team. I chose Newcastle University in the UK. I also identified additional partner organizations who could provide resources for the research, support my training and enhance my future career prospects. Contacting them even at this early stage, I arranged a secondment at the Victoria and Albert Museum Research Institute (V&A) in London (to be taken if the application was successful) and collaboration with Seven Stories, the UK's National Centre for Children's Books, in Newcastle. Then came the writing of the application, done in close and active collaboration with my prospective research supervisor. This took a couple of months of intense commitment on both sides.

I was notified that my application had been successful in January 2018, with the project due to start the following September. The application had been carefully scrutinized and evaluated, of course, and its strengths were identified as being the clarity with which I had written about a very specific gap in scholarship; a thorough account of the state-of-the-art in my chosen field and my demonstration of how my own approach to the topic would be different; a comprehensive explanation of the methodological and interdisciplinary aspects of the project; and the meticulousness of the work packages' structure and planning for milestones and deliverables. More generally, among the strengths of the application there was the credibility of my career possibilities, the two-way transfer of knowledge between me and the host institution, the training plan we had developed to support my development, and the fit with the supervisor.

In short, the positive evaluation the project gained would not have been possible without a strong match between the host and partner institution, the supervisor and myself, close collaboration between myself and my proposed supervisor, and the host institution's Research Funding Development office.

What did the project actually do? Much of my time was spent in careful research of my primary materials, asking how we define this genre; when, where and how these books were made; who produced them and for whom; and what was their role in cultural, publishing and visual history and their long-term influence. I established my research corpus by working closely with the Renier Collection at the V&A, the Opie Collection at the Bodleian Libraries in Oxford, Cambridge University Library, the British Library and the Cotsen Children's Library at Princeton University. But I had also promised other activities beyond my literary and book history research. In the absence of pre-existing European aggregators of children's books, the project envisioned the creation of a network of libraries, museums, and collections of kindred international institutions, providing an open, online venue useful for defining and agreeing on cataloguing standards and thesauri, meant to be a reference for further pan-European and transnational research. To implement the results of these collaborations and to provide institutions and future scholars with an easily retrievable, highly verified set of searchable data, an open access database was designed and launched one year after the project's kick off (https://www.picoboo.eu/). The outbreak of the Covid-19 pandemic strongly affected my plans, forcing the cancellation of planned exhibitions, conferences and several other dissemination activities. I had to amend my outputs, but was still able to accomplish my original objectives for public dissemination of my research through the flexibility or the collaborative relationships I had built up with international institutions holding collections of children's books.

To receive funding through such a competitive scheme, to be integrated into a wider research community across Europe and beyond, to be allowed the management and design of an independent, highly ambitious project, to gain access to materials and collections usually not available to the general public and to experience them behind-the-scenes: all this has been a milestone in my career and, beyond the scholarly research itself, has provided me with fundamental tools and skills, including effective writing of funding applications, project management, risk assessment, and networking skills across different communities.

7.1.3 Project funding

Academics already established in a university post will still often want to apply for funding. Sometimes this is simply necessary to pursue a desired course of research. For instance, a researcher may need to consult specific materials held in a distant archive. Or it might be that a project cannot be completed without a period of time dedicated to research or writing, free from normal academic duties. This is why fellowships and research leave schemes are so attractive: they can enable individual academics to 'buy themselves out' of their normal duties like teaching and administration, and/or provide funds for travel or research. Sometimes this kind of funding will be available internally within a university, but often it will require an application(s) to national and international funding agencies, or to particular institutions. The Internationalen Jugendbibliothek (International Youth Library) in Munich, for example, offers funding to around fifteen non-German scholars each year to support research, and academic exchange, in the field of international children's literature and illustration. Fellowships there can last between six weeks and three months, with a grant to cover living expenses. It can be difficult to find out about these opportunities. Many university libraries (particularly in North America) offer relatively small grants to encourage the use of their collections or facilities, and some scholarly societies (such as the Children's Literature Association[1]) support research with travel grants, bursaries and fellowships. Internet searches will identify many prospects, all of which will be competitive and each of which will have different selection criteria.

These fellowships and small grants almost always support individual scholarship, but some research is best carried out in teams. Networking grants are available from some national and international funding agencies, which are designed to stimulate the exchange of ideas, information and methods between researchers on a particular subject. A transnational project, for example, seeking to understand how migration and forced displacement is depicted and understood in children's books around the world would probably require many scholars to come together. A networking grant could pay workshops, seminars, conferences or similar activities, including the travel costs of participants. It might support the involvement of non-academics too: publishers, authors and illustrators, teachers, politicians and perhaps children

[1]https://www.childlitassn.org/awards-and-grants-overview

and young people themselves, some of whom might need to be compensated through the grant for the time they were contributing.

More ambitious still are large grants that support projects that involve a team of researchers and might last several years. Some national and international funding agencies have schemes that are entirely 'bottom-up', allowing researchers to choose their own topics and approach. Other schemes are 'top-down' and 'challenge-led', addressing a particular societal problem. Either kind will often be interdisciplinary or international in nature. It will usually be necessary to make a case that the project simply could not take place without the funding; for instance, because the outputs being planned require the collection of an enormous amount of data from many different places, or sophisticated uses of digital technology which will need to be built by data scientists or software engineers. And of course, these schemes, sometimes offering very large grants, are enormously competitive, requiring months or years of planning, including preliminary research, team-building and perhaps a pilot project. Actually writing the application itself can take months, requiring not only a compelling research proposal, but also a careful justification of the resources being requested, an account of why the team that has been assembled is exactly right for the project, an ambitious plan of how the research will impact on its users both academic and non-academic, letters of support from partners, data management plans for any digital work being undertaken, mitigation strategies for if things go wrong, and meticulous costings of all elements of the project. University research offices are set up to help with this, particularly the financial side of things.

This might seem a long way away from children's literature! But in fact, children's books can be a central part of many of our responses to major societal challenges, whether it is climate change, or the effects of a pandemic, or growing educational inequalities, or the societal effects of Artificial Intelligence. Funding agencies sometimes either explicitly or implicitly organize their schemes around the seventeen United Nations Societal

Development Goals (SDGs) agreed in 2015.[2] The most relevant of these to children's literature is '4: Quality Education', but it is not difficult to see how children's books and media could be an integral part of a response to many of the other global goals, including '5: Gender Equality', '13: Climate Action' or '16: Peace, Justice and Strong Institutions'. A glance through the directory of funded projects can provide inspiration, showing what kind of children's literature projects have been supported. On CORDIS, for example, which lists research projects funded by the European Union, are to be found 'Constructing Age for Young Readers', which looked at fiction for young readers, asking how age is conceptualized and communicated in cultural products, this having an effect on how children are taught in schools; or 'Our Mythical Childhood', which investigated the reception of classical antiquity in children's and young adults' contemporary culture across the world, so as better understand social, political and cultural transformation in a global context.[3] In Britain, the national funding agency (UKRI) has funded projects ranging from 'The Billiken Magazine Centenary Project: Children's Literature and Childhood in Argentina 1919-2019' and 'Decolonising Digital Childhoods: A pilot study towards enhanced participation and diversification in historical children's literature collections' to 'Reading Feelings: Does Reading Fiction Improve Children's Empathy and Pro-social Skills?'[4] Searches of projects funded by the Australian Research Council or the National Endowment for the Humanities in the United States, or elsewhere in the world, would reveal a similarly wide, and inspirational, array of approaches to using children's literature to address social challenges.

---

[2]https://www.globalgoals.org/
[3]https://cordis.europa.eu/
[4]https://gtr.ukri.org/

7.2 Engagement and impact

Only a few decades ago, universities were understood primarily as places dedicated to the education of students and to the development of knowledge for its own sake. Now, universities are equally interested in finding broader audiences for their scholarship, and in the *effects* of research. Taking research to audiences, and 'users', outside the university is usually called 'engagement'. Affecting and changing the world outside the university is usually called 'impact'. For instance, a lecture explaining research findings to an audience of the general public, schoolchildren or even a group with a professional interest in the research, would be engagement. So too would be a radio broadcast or television programme, a comic book or suite of TikTok videos that describes research findings, since the main aim of these is to disseminate knowledge and broaden its reach. On the other hand, if research led to a new toolkit for teachers to use in schools, or a series of lesson plans, it could count as impact, because the intention is to change teaching practice, and presumably to improve the education received by children. Likewise, a policy briefing, designed to change how an organization, or a business, or government, operated would usually count as impact, at least if it had the effect of changing policy. The line between engagement and impact can be blurred. Simply curating a museum exhibition on the basis of new research might count as engagement, since it could primarily be an exercise in dissemination of knowledge. But if the research were deployed in such a way that it changed the museum's policies or practice, or attracted a new set of visitors, or caused the museum to collect and display materials in new ways, it would be impact. Moreover, knowing when impact has occurred can be difficult. Is research really impactful if it were designed to change things, but actually didn't? To complicate matters further, other terms are sometimes used. When researchers work in collaboration with research users, often to develop impact, we might speak of 'Knowledge Exchange'. When new products, processes or services are developed based on research, particularly in a commercial context, the technical term 'Innovation' is often used. This is complicated but, in short, research 'impact' is the measurable effect – hopefully positive – that research has in the world.

Of course, research can still be valuable when it has no obvious impact. Knowledge for knowledge's sake, and academic freedom to investigate whatever seems most interesting and important in its own right, remain key principles of academic life in most universities. Also, 'blue-skies' or 'discovery' research, undertaken with no particular application in mind, can lead to benefits much later, which perhaps were never planned by the original researchers. Yet engagement and impact are important because they demonstrate the social, cultural or economic value beyond the scholarly value. This might be important to the individual researchers who want to see that their work has purpose. It is also increasingly central to the ways in which universities articulate their mission. Universities are also interested in impact because it helps them to justify investment. If it can be shown that universities contribute to the public good, it is easier to argue for public funding. Similarly, if a subject such as children's literature can show the beneficial effects it brings to society, it is easier to argue for support and investment within a university, or to make the case for external funding. As discussed above, as part of a funding application many grant-giving bodies will now require researchers to show what engagement, and more especially what impact, they hope to generate. National research assessment exercises also now generally attach a high worth to impact. In the UK, for example, the Research Excellence Framework (REF) exercise that takes place every few years currently accords 25 per cent of its overall score to research impact, which it seeks to measure by requiring each subject area to submit a series of case studies showing how their research has changed the world.

One might think that in some academic disciplines (such as clinical medicine or criminology) it would be easy to demonstrate research impact, whereas in others, including children's literature, it would be more difficult. But in fact, children's literature studies can be highly successful in showing how its research does good in the world. The REF exercise in the UK currently defines impact as an 'effect on, change or benefit to the economy, society, culture, public policy or services, health, the environment or quality of life, beyond academia'. It is a broad definition that allows impact to be on institutions, organizations, schools and businesses, but also on people. One could show that research has led to changes in people's health and well-being, their environment, their engagement with culture, their understanding of the world, their behaviour or attitudes, or their capacity to succeed (perhaps through education, or supporting their integration into society, or increasing their social capital). Importantly, these people can be children and young people as well as adults. Children's books themselves (along with other children's media) have often been produced to achieve exactly these kinds of benefits, so it is natural that children's literature studies should often also be intrinsically impactful. Indeed, it is not too difficult to construct strategies for ensuring that children's literature research can support children's literacy, or teaching more broadly; or can help organizations aiming at children's psychological development, or intercultural understanding; or can support the libraries, schools, publishers and government departments that themselves seek to connect young people with reading.

7.2.1 Examples of impact

As noted above, the UK's REF exercise invited the submission of 'Impact Case Studies' from each subject area. These case studies are now published in a searchable online directory (although without the 'score' they ultimately received in the exercise), and it is notable that many of them were based on research in children's literature studies.[5] Searching the directory for 'children's books' or 'children's literature' brings up thirty-two separate case studies, submitted by universities across the UK, for the 2021 exercise. They emanate from departments of English, Education, Modern Languages, History,

[5]See https://results2021.ref.ac.uk/impact. The case studies discussed in this section are all presented in more detail on this website.

and Art and Design, but also from units such as 'Psychology, Psychiatry and Neuroscience', 'Computer Science and Informatics' and 'Allied Health Professions'. Each entry describes what research underpins the impact, what impact is being claimed, and how the impact can be demonstrated. The case studies should not necessarily be regarded as models of good practice, but they do give an indication of the very broad kinds of impact that children's literature studies can generate.

Not surprisingly, some case studies make claims for impact on educational practice. At the Open University, research had been undertaken to design better approaches to encouraging reading for pleasure within primary schools. One finding was that teachers should be encouraged to develop better knowledge of what kinds of children's books and other reading materials were available to, and actually being used by, children. The researchers worked with over 300 schools to support the implementation of new strategies based on their findings. At the University of the West of England, researchers had published research that had interrogated the ideological alignments of children's literature, particularly in the ways reading can form children's attitudes to family and gender roles. This research enabled those involved in the project to work with educational professionals to show how teachers and children could be led to read more critically across a diverse range of texts. Impacts claimed included improved engagement and changes in pupils' behaviour. Another project, at Leeds University, sought to expand the teaching of Chinese in British schools, doing so in part by increasing the visibility of Chinese children's literature in translation, bringing benefits not only to schools and pupils, but also to translators and publishers.

Other projects aimed to reach children outside school settings. At Anglia Ruskin University, psychologists designed a new set of children's books and toys to teach parents to understand and support the emotional development of their pre-school children. Linguists at Coventry University sought to improve children's literacy attainment by embedding expertise in phonology and morphology into a new commercial reading scheme for four-to-seven-year-olds. Researchers at Birmingham City University worked with publishers to develop a new range of books using rhythmic reading activities to increase the reading proficiency of young children. Research at Northumbria University was used to generate greater appreciation of the role comics can have in supporting literacy, and indeed in changing the nature of modern comics themselves in areas like gender parity. Bournemouth University researchers sought to change attitudes around digital reading, particularly in the way it allows interactivity with books.

Participatory research involving children was part of several impact case studies (see Section 3.4.1). At Leeds Beckett University, for example, concern at the marginalization of creative arts in school curricula prompted researchers to explore the use of creative writing with children, leading to the establishment of a children's publishing venture that involved under-represented groups of children in the co-construction of children's books. At the University of Glasgow, researchers used their expertise to devise new ways of using children's books to support young people who had been displaced from their homes, specifically in Egypt and Mexico. Knowing that they would not easily have been able to reach those children directly, they worked in partnership with Non-Governmental Organizations and other agencies. Alternatively, researchers sometimes sought to achieve impact on children's publishing. At the Royal College of Art, for instance, a children's book author produced an experimental picturebook employing typography as a form of illustration, working with a publisher with the aim of expanding readership of children's books in inclusive and decolonial ways.

Collaboration with cultural institutions, such as museums or libraries, can also provide a powerful pathway to impact. At Newcastle University, research in children's literature was deployed to support the development of an independent organization called Seven Stories, which is the UK's National Centre for Children's Books. Seven Stories has a visitor centre, which mounts exhibitions and activities for children–and is amassing a major collection of books, manuscripts, original artwork and other material relating to British children's books from the 1930s to the present. In the 2014 REF exercise, the case study focused on the ways in which the work produced by a team of researchers in the Children's Literature Unit in the School of English Literature, Language and Linguistics helped to support the development of the Seven Stories Collection and supported the conceptualization and curation of exhibitions. This work was continued in the 2021 REF, with research designed to disrupt received understandings of the 'children's canon' being used to support Seven Stories' goals of expanding the diversity and inclusion of its Collection and its ambitions to expand and diversify its audiences. A separate case study, in the field of digital media, designed a new kind of digital tool to present Seven Stories' archival materials in interactive ways, using Augmented Reality technology to embed material from the collections into the landscape around the visitor centre.

It might be noted that most of these case studies have emerged from a body of work, rather than individual studies that focus on an individual book or author. This is not a requirement: a case study from Cardiff University was based on a single book which had uncovered the importance of Wales to the writing of Roald Dahl. The knowledge this had generated, it was claimed, was able to lead to a more central profile for Wales in the 'Roald Dahl 100' centenary celebrations that took place across the UK in 2016. Similarly, at Anglia Ruskin University, research on Lewis Carroll's *Alice* books, it was argued, had a significant influence on the celebrations of the 150th anniversary of the first publication of *Alice's Adventures in Wonderland*, with impacts being claimed through a programme of specially organized events, museum exhibitions, public lectures, theatrical and musical performances, and even citation in the US government's account of copyright legislation around *Alice*. Research on *Alice* at Queen Mary University of London, in particular on the importance of dress in Carroll's books, underpinned an even more expansive impact, including not only an exhibition at the Museum of Childhood, but also a concert suite for the London Symphony Orchestra and a textiles collection for the commercial company Liberty Art Fabrics.

7.2.2 Planning and achieving impact

It is certainly possible for strong impact to develop organically and inadvertently. You might also find out only in retrospect that your research has achieved impact. But if you know you want to achieve impact – and more especially if you know you will be asked to prove the impact your research has had – you would be well advised to plan it, starting as early in the process as you can. As will have been readily apparent from the examples given in the previous subsection, there are many different ways to achieve impact from research in children's literature, so naturally there are equally as many ways to generate it. Yet, some basic principles are relevant in most cases.

The best advice is to plan your impact from the outset. It will sometimes be possible to develop impact from research that has already been completed and published – and indeed the pathway from research to impact can often take years. But it is wise to build impact into your research plans from the start; in fact, you might want to decide on your next research project on the basis of the impact you expect it to achieve. Research and impact do not have to be thought of as different things, or as happening in different stages. It is perfectly reasonable to start a project by imagining the kinds of impacts you want to achieve, and then designing the research that would enable those impacts to happen. To take an example, perhaps you have learned that a museum will be opening a new gallery devoted to children's books in three years' time. You might aspire to help the museum staff to conceptualize and curate the exhibition. What research would you have to undertake in order to contribute most successfully? What is not already known about the subject of the exhibition? What questions will the museum staff be most interested in addressing, and what audiences will they be trying to reach? What format should your research findings take to have the most influence? The point is to think strategically and predictively about both your research and its potential impact. Indeed, just as you would be well advised to write a research plan before you begin a research project (Chapter 2), so you could write an impact plan; or better still, a single plan that takes into account both research and its impact.

Your impact plan should include a clear idea of who the beneficiaries of your research will be. Remember, impact means reaching a non-academic audience. So the beneficiaries, sometimes called 'stakeholders', might be members of the public, schools, cultural organizations, authors or illustrators, publishers or other commercial companies and so on. You should be as specific as possible, although recognizing that plans can change and new opportunities emerge. So if you are thinking of schoolchildren, which age groups will you be trying to reach, and in which schools? A crucial point to remember is that you need to be thinking about potential *beneficiaries*, not merely *audiences*. However interesting your research might be, the point of impact is that the research should change (and ideally improve) the way things are done, rather than merely being absorbed or even admired.

It is worth noting that impacts can be indirect as well as direct. For instance, your research could be about innovative uses of digital editions of picturebooks, and your ambition could be to improve the ways in which teachers use them in their lessons. Rather than designing your research and your publications so that they are read and used directly by teachers however, you could design a plan that communicated your findings to teacher training institutions (educating future generations of teachers), or to professional bodies for teachers (that spread good practice), or perhaps to the commercial companies that produce the digital picturebooks (to embed advice on use, or new functionality, in their products). Or you might want to plan to do all these things. The ultimate beneficiaries here would be the children in school, but there would have been several steps in this 'chain' of impact.

Having defined your stakeholders and beneficiaries, you should engage with them at the earliest opportunity. This is important because they can themselves tell you what they most need from your research, which will naturally make your research more effective in generating impact. You could ask businesses what their commercial needs are. Or you could ask a community to share their most pressing concerns. Popular ways to do this include holding meetings and workshops with your designated partners, attending conferences or community events where you know that your stakeholders will be present, conducting interviews, surveys or questionnaires, but community consultation can also be done digitally (through online reading groups, say). Once you have consulted with your stakeholders, you can design your research to ask the questions, and find the answers, that address their needs. When you engage with your research users like this, you are co-producing your research, a method which is becoming increasingly common.

Co-production with your stakeholders is a kind of participatory research that has some practical and ethical complications, covered elsewhere in this book (Sections 3.4 and 3.5). But when you are trying to generate impact, it is a much more effective strategy than you deciding on your research questions and methods yourself, and then just throwing it out to its potential beneficiaries and hoping they will find it useful. It is critical to build relationships with your stakeholders on a basis of trust and mutual benefit, and perhaps to find ways of recompensing your partners for their time. This helps in the short term, but sustaining good relationships for the full duration of the project, or over the course of many projects, will bring other dividends. If you set up a Young People's Advisory Group, for example, its members can help you design the research and offer advice on what formats and media to use for communicating your findings (text or infographic; print or video; which social media your target audience uses most?) and how to reach other potential users. When it comes to gathering evidence of your impact, they may be willing to provide testimonials or introduce you to other communities of users.

Other key points for your impact planning will be how you will reach your potential beneficiaries and how you can ensure that the people you hope to reach will actually act on what you have to tell them. There are many ways to gain traction for your research. You could organize stakeholder workshops, present at conferences held by professional bodies, produce films, write policy documents: the best strategy will depend on the type of audience you are trying to reach. You can be ambitious here, but you also need to be realistic. How long would it take to produce the impact you would like? How much will it cost? Just as with a research project, your impact plan needs to be feasible. You might want to think of a mitigation strategy too: what would you do if your initial plans become impossible to achieve? You should also think carefully about whether the activities you are planning will be able to deliver real impact.

Let us suppose, for example, that you have been researching children's use of local public libraries. Perhaps your research has proved that libraries that remain open for longer at weekends, or that provide creche facilities for younger children, or that schedule associated but non-core activities, are more appealing to families, and thus encourage children's reading. You might write a policy document setting out your evidence and your recommendations, with the intention that it will be read at local government level and acted upon. It would be important to write the document in a concise and punchy way, unlike the thesis or research article on which it was based, which was intended for an academic audience. You could employ someone to write the report in the format the local government officials are used to seeing, or with attractive photography and striking infographics. This is all good, but still, how would you ensure that your policy briefing actually gets read, rather than being sent out, received but ignored? Maybe you would need to host an event to which you would invite the policymakers, so that you could convince them of the importance of the work? Perhaps a social media campaign would be useful? Or perhaps you should try to reach the policymakers via some 'brokers', maybe via a lobby group, or political figures, or a professional librarians' body, who can transmit your case to those with the power to actually change library policy. If you are hoping to change policy, it is also worth thinking about the tone in which you present your recommendations. You might have strong opinions, which may be driven by your own emotional or ideological responses, but it is probably more effective, from the point of view of impact, to present your research as objectively as you can, with your recommendations clearly driven by the evidence you have collected.

The final challenge is often how you can *prove* your impact. You will not want to find yourself in the position of having to collect evidence of impact long after it has happened, so you need to plan for evidence collection from the beginning, and then collect documentation as you go along. You will want to keep track of the details of what you have done: for instance, how many people attended your events, and what did they think of them? It will be much more difficult to obtain this testimony months or years later, so you will want to retain letters and emails, as well as photos and media coverage. Search engine analytics or social media posts can be useful to support your case. And testimonials of the effects of your research are often used, whether from individuals or organizations. Be wary, however, for testimonials are not always the strongest kind of proof, since it could be argued that they are the result merely of friendly collaboration. The best indicators of impact will be from clearly independent and unbiassed sources. They will be credible because they are verifiable, and perhaps because they clearly identify a baseline from which the change has happened. Above all, your evidence should clearly demonstrate *change*, not just that you attracted an audience for your research. Citation of your work in policy documents, whether from agencies or companies or government is often very convincing. Ideally, multiple sources of evidence will corroborate the impact you are claiming. Often cases for impact are strongest if they can show substantial change over a sustained period, or over a wide geographical range. But highly localized and small-scale impacts can be highly significant if they bring deep benefits to even a small number of people. In the end, you may find that you have to spend as much time collecting and presenting your evidence of impact as you did actually undertaking the underlying research. To that end, this chapter concludes with an example of how impact was planned, executed and will be measured.

7.2.3 Case study by Elisa Marazzi

Between 2019 and 2022, I carried out the project *Children and Transnational Popular Print, 1700–1900*. Funded by the European Union under the Marie

Skłodowka-Curie scheme, it was aimed at re-assessing the role played by cheaply printed items (such as illustrated broadsides, chapbooks, almanacs) within children's literature in Western Europe between 1700 and 1900. The relevance of such items in terms of access to literacy, self-teaching and reading opportunities in past European societies had been vaguely acknowledged by scholarship for decades, but no in-depth study had been carried out. My project was designed to address this gap.

The project's main academic aim was to increase understanding among scholars of the extent, multifariousness and significance of popular print for children and its role in literacy and knowledge circulation in the early modern period. I planned to do this using traditional methods for dissemination: conference presentations and publications. In terms of impact, the project has two main objectives:

1. To raise awareness among professionals (in libraries, museums) of the relevance of cheap print, which, while preserved in their collections, is seldom the object of exhibition, exploitation or promotion;
2. To reach out to the general public in order to challenge stereotypes regarding literacy and access to knowledge by ordinary people in the past.

The most successful impact outputs were the two exhibitions I curated. These exhibitions were designed differently from one another, partly because of the different partners I was working with, and partly because of the different outcomes I sought.

The first of these exhibitions was called *Bibliothèques bleues* and took place at the Centre de conservation et de ressources (CCR) du Musée des civilisations de l'Europe et de la Méditerranée (MUCEM). This is a major museum in Marseille, France. I co-curated the exhibition with Sophie Bernillon, head librarian at the CCR at MUCEM. I had been advised to liaise with this institution by academic colleagues who identified its collections of cheap print to be interesting and little exploited. At the time of my funding application, I made the first contact by email, explaining what the aims of my project were, and what kind of co-production I was hoping for. Their agreement enabled me to state in my application that the institution had agreed in principle to the partnership. Once we started to work together, our first task was to compare and exchange our expertise, and to discuss the most relevant items in their collections for our purposes. This happened initially by email. I searched for items through both catalogues and scans provided by the CCR, and then discussed my finds with the co-curator. A one-month stay, funded by the scheme as a secondment, was initially planned in order to carry out this task, although the Covid-19 pandemic meant it was downsized to one intense week, during which we were able to make the final choices, singling out around 100 items from the CCR collections to show the different possible intersections between cheap print and children's literature in the French history of books and prints. Thereafter, online meetings were held with administrators and the exhibitions production team at MUCEM. A launch event was planned, alongside with the inclusion of the exhibition in the rich calendar of school visits routinely held at CCR. All this led to the following results:

- Researchers in the field were invited to present at the online launch of the exhibition in April 2021. The invitation inspired them to undertake new research on the intersections between cheap print and children's literature, and also to think about what evidence they had regarding how children consumed the kinds of items showcased.
- Working alongside the collection's curator made it possible for MUCEM to better understand the new knowledge created by the project and how it concerned CCR's collections. In the long term, it should be possible to assess whether this collaboration has led to changes in the CCR's policies in terms of exploitation of their resources.

It is difficult to assess what this exhibition achieved in terms of public outreach, as the timing was unfortunate: it was held during the Covid-19 pandemic, and exhibitions in France had to close their doors just days after the exhibition's launch. However, a partnership with an institution that is strong in terms of outreach makes it possible to exploit its communication channels (social media, press office) and engagement activities, both key to success in terms of societal impact, as the following case will show better.

The second exhibition to come out of my project was called *Stampe per crescere* and was held at the Museo Per Via, Pieve Tesino (Italy). The venue was carefully chosen as the museum, in a small village in northern Italy, is devoted to the history of local pedlars who marketed illustrated broadsides across the Alps. The museum offered its premises and infrastructure in order to showcase its own work alongside items that my project was able to secure on loan from different collections. I selected fifty items from international collections, including digitized images from Princeton's Cotsen Children's Library and the Rijksmuseum Amsterdam. Museo Per Via's strong ties with the local community made it possible for the museum to attract the attention of general audiences as well as specialists in the field with pre-existing interests in the history of literacy.

To enhance the exhibition's impact, I worked with the museum on several specific activities:

- A printed catalogue available for purchase both in the museum and online, and sent to relevant scholars and institutions;
- A public talk held during an annual festival promoted by the local community and carefully designed to be enjoyed by non-experts, as well as being accompanied by buskers' performances in the spirit of the festival;
- Guided tours with the curator on the festival's launch day;
- Training session for museum guides.

To measure the impact of the exhibition, we recorded attendance and visitors' understanding of what they had seen by using the methods routinely employed by the museum.

Ultimately, I found that my impact activities were as crucial to my project as the more scholarly work. I learned the importance of embedding outreach events in the calendars of institutions that are already expecting to reach public audiences. Working in partnership with these institutions, my project was able to achieve much greater success in highlighting the central place that writing for children has occupied in the long history of cheap print in Europe.

As well as undertaking and writing up research, the scholars of today and the future have to become experts in raising funding, securing real-world partners, producing innovative and wide-reaching outputs and generally ensuring that at least some of their research has impact outside the immediate academic community. These added dimensions to research are demanding, but can also be rewarding. What could be more different from writing a book or article that may be read by just a few people than, say, using children's literature expertise to help develop a major exhibition, a policy-changing initiative or a project for young people undergoing challenging medical treatments?

Afterword

Keep on going by Emily Murphy

While institutions, organizations and individuals may offer advice on how to get started on a career in children's literature studies, we hope that having that advice bound together in a single book, as it is here, will have lasting value. One reason for this is that it will enable and encourage you not to make ad hoc decisions, but to think strategically from the beginning about what you need to do to be an active participant in the field. No one can tell you the value of the path you have chosen, or how far you are willing to go to reach your career goals. For myself, this meant two international moves, and a lot of personal expense and sacrifice, to land a permanent job that gave me the freedom to pursue my interest and expertise in global children's literature. Indeed, had my younger self known the turn my life would take by moving across the globe for a temporary position as a writing instructor in China, I would not have believed it. It is nearly a decade later, and I am still living and working overseas, though now in England as Senior Lecturer in Children's Literature. As part of my university position, I also continue to build on that early experience through international partnerships with children's literature programmes around the world. If you persevere, as I chose to do, you will require stamina, resilience and grit, and you must be prepared for hard work. There are no sinecures. But as Chapter 4's discussion of 'Challenges and Barriers' outlines, success is often only partially down to hard work: to make the playing field more even, sometimes you must change the rules of the game. Put another way, you need to find ways to communicate the value of the work you are passionate about to others who may not share your enthusiasm.

You *can* take control of building your professional value. In the early stages of your career, you will focus much of your attention on developing the competencies needed to carry out your professional responsibilities. These may include such skills as grant-writing, oral presentations and teaching. However, once you have taken these first steps and feel confident in the areas of expertise required for your job within children's literature studies, you will need to find ways to go beyond the basics – indeed, it is worthwhile considering this even at an early stage as it will help set you apart when you look for your first position once you have completed your studies. Such a task requires thinking about the professional climate: What can you give that will help nurture the growth of children's literature studies? How will your contributions translate into meaningful benefits for those who you hope will employ you? The answers to these two questions are not always, indeed are often not, the same. Careful research and a lot of listening are required to identify the best path forward that draws on your own strengths and interests. In time you may even receive financial support from an employer to try put your ideas into action, but at all stages it's important to investigate a broad range of paths that might help you grow in ways that will fulfil your career goals and develop your professional value.

As you consider different ways to build this value, it is worth exploring non-traditional options that can expand your skill set. If you are interested in impact and engagement work, as covered in Chapter 7, then focusing on building relationships with partners outside of academia, including children and young people (see Chapter 3), can be a rewarding use of your time. You can find allies in these partnerships, as well as long-lasting friends who can help encourage you when you hit a rough point in your career. How your skills evolve will depend on your needs and values, but even something as simple as volunteering at a local community youth centre, could be a way to develop yourself and give back to your community in a way that aligns with your goals and interests. As an example, if you are determined to win a big national or international grant, but need to gain skills in working with younger children or youth, then taking short courses that focus on specialized teaching methods such as Philosophy for Children (P4C) could be beneficial, and even enrich other areas of your professional life, if you work in a university or other higher/further education setting. No matter how you aim to develop your professional value, the key is to keep allowing yourself to grow in ways that are rewarding and fulfilling to you.

If you have read this far into our handbook, then you probably have the determination to keep going in the field of children's literature studies. Perhaps you have already secured a coveted funded position as a postgraduate student or are further along in your career – working at postdoctoral level or even as a junior colleague in a permanent post. Regardless of how far down the professional path you have gone, at certain moments you are sure to stop and wonder if all your effort will pay off. In fact, perhaps the most shocking thing to junior colleagues is how much you must *still* work to prove yourself even once you have obtained a permanent position. You should remember in these times that you are part of a field that has worked tirelessly to communicate its value. The rising numbers in organizations such as the International Research Society for Children's Literature (IRSCL) and the Children's Literature Association (ChLA), along with the increasing opportunities for support and mentorship, is inspiring, and it is a direct result of the hard work of those who started out exactly where you were many years ago. Reflecting on how the influential figures within our field worked to communicate the value of children's literature studies is often helpful in reflecting on your own path: what legacy will you leave behind when you reach the end of your career?

When I think about these success stories, one that I recall again and again is that of Dr Lena de Grummond, who was responsible for the University of Southern Mississippi's internationally recognized collection of children's books and original manuscripts. When de Grummond was setting out to build her collection of children's books in the 1960s, she wrote hundreds of letters to children's authors and illustrators, asking them to send her their original manuscripts, dummies, sketches, and any other materials that could help her library science students learn about the publication process. She used the line, 'If you put your materials in the trash, please send that basket to us'. And guess what? They did! Authors and illustrators as famous as H. A. Rey not only sent de Grummond a few bits: they sent boxes upon boxes of original materials. This was at a time when not only others outside of the field of children's literature studies failed to value such items, but even those working within the profession held them in scant regard. They were often incredulous that anyone would find value in the preliminary work. De Grummond began the work of changing that perception. She helped others see value in something that she found important, and she used it to inspire and change the lives of the students she taught. So, if you do find yourself flagging, feeling the drain of the pressures of academia, or frustrated that your career is not taking off as fast as you'd like, keep looking for ways to inspire others, or change how they look at your niche within the field. How can you help others see the value in what you value? How can you, in doing so, find value in yourself. And remember, as this book begins by setting out in Chapter 1, children's literature studies is one of the most versatile areas in the arts, humanities and social sciences. Your decision to study it is the first and most important step in building a career in this dynamic, wide-ranging and pervasive field.

WORKS CITED

Adolphs, S. (2006), *Introducing Electronic Text Analysis: A Practical Guide for Language and Literary Studies*, London: Routledge.

Adolphs, S. and D. Knight, eds (2020), *The Routledge Handbook of English Language and Digital Humanities*, London: Routledge.

Anderson, C. C. (1984), *Style in Children's Literature: A Comparison of Passages From Books for Adults and for Children*, Kingston: University of Rhode Island.

Arnold, T. and L. Tilton (2023), *Distant Viewing: Computational Exploration of Digital Images*, Cambridge: MIT Press.

Austin, S. and A. M. Wainscott (2021), 'Children's Literature as a Front in the War on Terror: Ineffective Policy, Ineffective Literature', *International Research in Children's Literature*, 14 (1): 52–66.

Balagopalan, S. (2014), *Inhabiting "Childhood": Children, Labour, and Schooling in Postcolonial India*, London: Palgrave Macmillan.

Bamman, D., et al. (2014), 'A Bayesian Mixed Effects Model of Literary Character', *Proceedings of the 52nd Annual Meeting of the Association for Computational Linguistics*, 370–9, Baltimore: Association for Computational Linguistics.

Bang, M. (1991), *Picture This: How Pictures Work*, Boston: Little Brown.

Bansal, S. (2017), *Ultimate Guide to Understand & Implement Natural Language Processing (with Codes in Python), Analytics Vidhya.* https://www.analyticsvidhya.com/blog/2017/01/ultimate-guide-to-understand-implement-natural-language-processing-codes-in-python/ (accessed 26 March 2024).

Beckett, S. (2009), *Crossover Fiction: Global and Historical Perspectives*, London: Routledge.

Benjamin, R. (2019), *Race After Technology: Abolitionist Tools for the New Jim Code*, Cambridge: Polity Press.

Best, S. and S. Marcus (2009), 'Surface Reading: An Introduction', *Representations*, 108 (1): 1–21. https://doi.org/10.1525/rep.2009.108.1.1.

Bishop, R. S. (1990), 'Mirrors, Windows, and Sliding Glass Doors', *Perspectives: Choosing and Using Books for the Classroom*, 6 (3): ix–xi.

Burrell, J. (2016), 'How the Machine "Thinks": Understanding Opacity in Machine Learning Algorithms', *Big Data & Society*, 3 (1). https://doi.org/10.1177/2053951715622512.

Bradford, C. et al. (2008), *New World Orders in Contemporary Children's Literature*, Basingstoke: Palgrave Macmillan.

Brown, N. (2017), *The Children's Film: Genre, Nation, and Narrative*, New York: Columbia University Press.

Bruhn, J. et al., eds (2014), *Adaptation Studies: New Challenges, New Directions*, London: Bloomsbury.

Carey, J. (2019), *Judith Kerr*, London: Thames and Hudson.

Caracciolo, M. (2022), *Slow Narratives and Nonhuman Materialities*, Lincoln, NE: University of Nebraska Press.
Cheney, K. (2018), 'Decolonizing Childhood Studies: Overcoming Patriarchy and Prejudice in Child-Related Research and Practice', in S. Spyros, R. Rosen and D. T. Cook (eds), *Reimagining Childhood Studies*, 91–105, London: Bloomsbury Academic.
Crawford, K. (2021), *Atlas of AI: Power, Politics, and the Planetary Costs of Artificial Intelligence*, Yale: Yale University Press.
Cross, A., et al. (2019), 'Digital Curation, AustLit, and Australian Children's Literature', *International Research in Children's Literature*, 12 (1): 1–17.
Dixon, B. (1977), *Catching Them Young, Vol 1: Sex, Race and Class in Children's Fiction*, London: Pluto Press.
Dixon, B. (1977), *Catching Them Young, Vol 2: Political Ideas in Children's Fiction*, London: Pluto Press.
Drucker, J. (2017), 'Why Distant Reading Isn't', *PMLA/Publications of the Modern Language Association of America*, 132 (3): 628–35. https://doi.org/10.1632/pmla.2017.132.3.628.
Dumas, M. J. (2014), '"Losing an Arm": Schooling as a Site of Black Suffering', *Race Ethnicity and Education*, 17 (1): 1–29.
Dusinberre, J. (1987), *Alice to the Lighthouse: Children's Books and Radical Experiments in Art*, Basingstoke: Macmillan.
Edmond, J. (2018), 'Managing Uncertainty in the Humanities: Digital and Analogue Approaches', *TEEM'18: Proceedings of the Sixth International Conference on Technological Ecosystems for Enhancing Multiculturality*, 840–4, Spain: Salamanca.
Eve, P. M. (2019), *Close Reading with Computers: Textual Scholarship, Computational Formalism, and David Mitchell's Cloud Atlas*, Stanford: Stanford University Press. https://doi.org/10.21627/9781503609372.
Faire, R. (2021), 'The Political Role of Philippine Children and Young People as Represented in Youth Fiction', *International Research in Children's Literature*, 14 (1): 39–51.
Falconer, R. (2009), *The Crossover Novel: Contemporary Children's Fiction and its Adult Readership,* New York and London: Routledge.
Fielder, B. (2019), '"Before the Brownies" Book', *The Lion and the Unicorn,* 43 (2): 159–71.
Fitzhugh, L. (1964), *Harriet the Spy*, New York: Harper and Row.
Fox, G. et al., eds (1976 [1973]), *Writers, Critics and Children*, London: Heinemann.
Freire, P. and D. Macedo (2005), *Literacy: Reading the Word and the World*, London: Routledge.
Gavin, M. (2019), 'Is There a Text in My Data? On Counting Words', *Journal of Cultural Analytics*, 5 (1). https://doi.org/10.22148/001c.11830.
Giddens, E. (2017), 'Distant Reading and Children's Literature', in C. Beauvais and M. Nikolajeva (eds), *The Edinburgh Companion to Children's Literature*, 305–13, Edinburgh: Edinburgh University Press.
Gonzalez, J. (2001), *Harvest of Empire,* New York: Penguin.
Griffin, M. (2018), *Once Upon a Genre: Distant Reading, the Newbery Medal, and the Affordances of Interdisciplinary Paradigms for Understanding Children's Literature*, Tampa: University of South Florida.

Haverals, W. and V. Joosen (2021), 'Constructing Age in Children's Literature: A Digital Approach to Guus Kuijer's Oeuvre', *The Lion and the Unicorn*, 45 (1): 25–45. https://doi.org/10.1353/uni.2021.0002.

Haverals, W., et al. (2022), 'A Style for Every Age: A Stylometric Enquiry into Crosswriters for Children, Adolescents and Adults', *Language and Literature*, 3 (1): 62–84.

Hermansson, Casie E. (2019), *Filming the Children's Book: Adapting Metafiction*, Edinburgh: Edinburgh University Press.

Hunt, P., ed. (1990 [1971]), *Children's Literature: The Development of Criticism*, London and New York: Routledge.

Hunt, P., ed. (1991), *Criticism, Theory and Children's Literature*, Oxford: Blackwell.

Hunt, P., ed. (1995), 'How Not to Read a Children's Book', *Children's Literature in Education*, 26 (2): 231–40.

Hodgson, J. (2023), 'Historians, Emotions, and Children's Trauma in the Archives', *Qualitative Inquiry*. https://doi.org/10.1177/10778004231200265.

Immerwahr, D. (2021), *How to Hide an Empire*, New York: Macmillan.

Jänicke, S., et al. (2015), 'On Close and Distant Reading in Digital Humanities: A Survey and Future Challenges', *EuroVis 2015*, 83–103, Cahliari, Italy: Eurographics Association. https://doi.org/10.2312/eurovisstar.20151113.

Jiménez-Roman, M. and J. Flores (2009), *The AfroLatin@ Reader*, Durham, NC: Duke University Press.

Joosen, V. (2021), 'Research in Action: Constructing Age for Young Readers', *International Research in Children's Literature*, 14 (3): 252–68.

Joosen, V., et al. (2023), *Age in David Almond's Oeuvre: A Multi-Method Approach to Studying Age and the Life Course in Children's Literature*, London: Routledge. https://doi.org/10.4324/9781003369608.

Juola, P. (2023), 'How a Computer Program Helped Show J.K. Rowling Write A Cuckoo's Calling', *Scientific American*. https://www.scientificamerican.com/article/how-a-computer-program-helped-show-jk-rowling-write-a-cuckoos-calling/ (accessed 23 April 2024).

Karsdorp, F. and L. Fonteyn (2019), 'Cultural Entrenchment of Folktales is Encoded in Language', *Palgrave Communications*, 5 (1): 25.

Karsdorp, F., M. Kestemont and A. Riddell (2021), *Humanities Data Analysis: Case Studies with Python*, Princeton: Princeton University Press.

Kestemont, M. and L. Herman (2019), 'Can Machines Read (Literature)?', *Umanistica Digitale* (5): 1–12. https://doi.org/10.6092/ISSN.2532-8816/8511.

Kerr, J. (2013), *Creatures: A Celebration of the Life and Work of Judith Kerr*, London: HarperCollins.

King, H. (2022), '"Children My Age Should Be Reading Books Like Journey to Jo'burg": Patterns of Anti-Racist Reading in Archived Reader Responses', *International Research in Children's Literature*, 15 (3): 264–78.

King, H. (2023), *We are the Gift of Life' : Exploring the Political Potential of Childhood Reading through the Work of Beverley Naidoo*, PhD thesis, Newcastle upon Tyne: Newcastle University.

Leitch, T., ed. (2017), *The Oxford Handbook of Adaptation Studies*, New York: Oxford University Press.

Lerer, S. (2008), *Children's Literature: A Reader's History from Aesop to Harry Potter*, Chicago and London: University of Chicago Press.

Martí, J. (1891), 'Our America', *El Partido Liberal*, Mexico City.

McDowell, M. (1976 [1973]), 'Fiction for Children and Adults: Some Essential Differences', in G. Fox et al., (eds), *Writers, Critics and Children*, 140–56, London: Heinemann.

Meeusen, M. (2020), *Children's Books on the Big Screen*, Jackson: University Press of Mississippi.

Moretti, F. (2013), *Distant Reading*, London: Verso Books.

O'Sullivan, E. (2005 [2000]), *Comparative Children's Literature*, London: Routledge.

Pearson, M. (9 August, 1938), 'A Married Name as a Business Handicap', *Sydney Morning Herald (Woman's Supplement)*, 12.

'Recommended Preservation Formats for Electronic Records' (2017), Smithsonian Institution Archives. https://siarchives.si.edu/what-we-do/digital-curation/recommended-preservation-formats-electronic-records (accessed 7 January 2024).

Reynolds, K. (2007), *Radical Children's Literature: Future Visions and Aesthetic Transformations*, Basingstoke: Palgrave Macmillan.

Reynolds, K. (1998), 'Publishing Practices and the Practicalities of Publishing', in K. Reynolds and N. Tucker (eds), *Children's Book Publishing in Britain Since 1945*, 20–41, Aldershot: Scolar Press.

Reese, D. (2006–), 'American Indians in Children's Literature', *website*, https://americanindiansinchildrensliterature.blogspot.com.

Roman, M. J. and J. Flores (2009), *The AfroLatin@ Reader*, Durham, N.C.: Duke University Press.

Rosa, J. and N. Flores (2017), 'Unsettling Race and Language: Toward a Raciosociolingusitic Perspective', *Language in Society*, 46 (5): 621–47.

Samuels, E. (2017), 'Six Ways of Looking at Crip Time', *Disability Studies Quarterly*, 37 (3). https://doi.org/10.18061/dsq.v37i3.5824.

Sanchez-Eppler, K. (2013), 'In the Archives of Childhood', in A. M. Duane (ed.), *The Children's Table: Childhood Studies and the Humanities*, 213–37, Georgia: University of Georgia Press.

Saguisag, L. (2018), *Incorrigibles and Innocents: Constructing Childhood and Citizenship in Progressive Era Comics*, New Brunswick, N.J.: Rutgers University Press.

Schofield, T. et al. (2016), 'Magical Realism and Augmented Reality: Designing Apps with Childr3en in a Cultural Institution', *DIS 19: Proceedings of the 2019 Designing Interactive Systems* Conference, San Jose: ACM Digital Library. https://doi.org/10.1145/3322276.332293.

Schreibman, S. et al., eds (2016), *A New Companion to Digital Humanities*, Oxford: Wiley-Blackwell.

Shavit, Z. (2009 [1986]), *Poetics of Children's Literature*, Athens: University of Georgia Press.

Slater, K. (2017), 'WeNeedDiverseScholars: A Forum', *The Lion and the Unicorn*, 41 (1): 93–103.

Smith, P. (2020), 'Paddington Bear and the Erasure of Difference', *Children's Literature Association Quarterly*, 45 (1): 25–42.

Stover, D. (2024), 'Digital Humanities and Children's Literature', in C. Nelson et al. (eds), *The Routledge Companion to Children's Literature and Culture*, 69–79, London: Routledge.

Stone, L. (2022), 'Childhood Exile Drawn and Redrawn: Judith Kerr's and Tomi Ungerer's Written and Pictorial Texts from and about the Nazi Era', PhD thesis, Newcastle University: Newcastle upon Tyne.

Street, D. (1982), 'An Overview of Commercial Filmic Adaptation of Children's Fiction', *Children's Literature Association Quarterly*, 7 (3): 13–17.

Superle, M. (2010), 'Imagining the New Indian Girl: Representations of Indian Girlhood in *Keeping Corner* and *Suchitra and the Ragpicker*', *Papers: Explorations into Children's Literature*, 20 (1): 31–40.

Tamboukou, M. (2017), 'Archival Rhythms: Narrativity in the Archive', in N. Moore et al. (eds), *The Archive Project: Archival Research in the Social Sciences*, 7–96, London and New York: Routledge.

Thomas, E. E. (2016), 'Stories Still Matter: Rethinking the Role of Diverse Children's Literature Today', *Language Arts*, 94 (2): 112–9.

Thomas, E. E. and A. Stornaiuolo (2016), 'Restorying the Self: Bending Toward Textual Justice', *Harvard Educational Review*, 86 (3): 313–38.

Thomas, E. E. and A. Stornaiuolo (2019), *The Dark Fantastic: Race and the Imagination from Harry Potter to The Hunger Games*, New York: New York University Press.

Townsend, J. R. (1990, [1971]), 'Standards of Criticism for Children's Literature', in P. Hunt (ed.), *Children's Literature: The Development of Criticism*, 57–70, London and New York: Routledge.

Tucker, N. (2006), 'Depressive Stories for Children', *Children's Literature in Education*, 37 (3): 199–210.

Tucker, N. (1976), *Suitable for Children? Controversies in Children's Literature*, Berkeley and Los Angeles, CA: University of California Press.

Ungerer, T. (1998), *Tomi: A Childhood Under the Nazis*, Dublin: TomiCo.

Vasconcelos, J. (1997 [1925]), *The Cosmic Race* (trans. Didier T. Jaen), Baltimore: Johns Hopkins University Press.

Wall, B. (1991), *The Narrator's Voice: The Dilemma of Children's Fiction*, London: Macmillan.

Walsh, J. P. (1977 [1971]), 'The Rainbow Surface', in M. Meek, A. Warlow and G. Barton (eds), *The Cool Web: The Patterns of Children's Reading*, 192–5, London: The Bodley Head.

Webb, J. (2018), 'Alice and Paddington: Digital Migrants from Book to Film', in I.B Kalla et al. (eds), *On the Fringes of Literature and Digital Media Culture*, 159–70, Amsterdam: Brill.

Weinreich, T. (2000), *Children's Literature – Art or Pedagogy?*, Copenhagen: Rothskilde University Press.

Wevers, M. and T. Smits (2020), 'The Visual Digital Turn: Using Neural Networks to Study Historical Images', *Digital Scholarship in the Humanities*, 35 (1): 194–207.

Willer, T., (2017), *L'Art de l'Enfance: Tomi Ungerer 1935–1953* [Childhood Art: Tomi Ungerer 1935–1953], Strasbourg: Musées de la Ville de Strasbourg.

Wojcik-Andrews, I. (2000), *Children's Films: History, Ideology, Pedagogy, Theory*, New York: Garland.

Xie, S. (1999), 'Rethinking the Identity of Cultural Otherness: The Discourse of Difference as an Unfinished Project', in R. McGillis (ed.), *Voices of the Other: Children's Literature and the Postcolonial Context*, 16–37, London: Routledge.

Zhu, Ziqiang (2000), *Chinese Children's Literature and China's Modernization*, Zhejiang: Zhejiang Children's Literature Publishing House.

INDEX

www.ingramcontent.com/pod-product-compliance
Lightning Source LLC
Chambersburg PA
CBHW071602030726
47593CB00001BA/278

* 9 7 8 1 3 5 0 3 7 7 4 9 3 *